Shameless Promos for
Risky is the New Safe

They Loved It—You Might Too!

"This is your go-to business page-turner! Randy's forward-thinking concepts embody my own business ideals for driving success within organizations: take risks, no one's going to die!"
    —**Jeffrey Hayzlett**, global business celebrity and
    bestselling author of *Sometime Cowboy*

"This remarkable, fast-paced book opens your mind and imagination to the incredible opportunities that appear around you when you change your perspective."
    —**Brian Tracy**, author of *The Power of Self-Confidence*

"Holy crap, I love this book! It's smart, entertaining, and best of all, made me re-think my life and my business. That's a winning combination I find irresistible. Don't hesitate to buy this book and put it to use in every aspect of your life."
    —**Larry Winget**, five-time NYT/WSJ bestselling author,
    including the #1 bestseller, *Shut Up, Stop
    Whining & Get A Life!*

"Read this book. But, before you do, suspend what you already believe is true about the way the world is and operates. You are about to learn what 'critical thinking' is all about, why risky indeed is the new (and perhaps, only) safe, and how it can make you wiser and more prosperous. The good news is that—in typical Randy Gage style—it will be fun, entertaining, and just sarcastic enough to keep you riveted to every page. Get out your pen and highlighter . . . you're gonna need it!"
    —**Bob Burg**, co-author of *The Go-Giver* and
    author of *Endless Referrals*

"Couldn't take my eyes off this great freaking book! *Risky is the New Safe* is a combination of Buffet, Springsteen, Rand, and Patton. Randy Gage is the ranking intellect of prosperity in our time, and only Luddites will ignore him. He has, yet again, written of the promise of abundance, the appeal of change, and the vast value of new and emerging relationships. There's nothing risky about buying this book except forgetting to do anything else while you're engrossed in it."
—**Alan Weiss,** PhD, author of *The Consulting Bible* and
Thrive: Stop Wishing Your Life Away!

"Relevant, challenging, and thought-provoking. This book is a must-read for entrepreneurs."
—**Ken Dychtwald,** PhD, author of *A New Purpose: Redefining Money, Family, Work, Retirement, and Success*

"*Risky is the New Safe* is eye opening, mind blowing, and gut real. It gives you a step-by-step blueprint for succeeding in today's new world. If you are an entrepreneur, a business person, or want to create wealth in your life you HAVE to read this book!"
—**T. Harv Eker,** author of the *New York Times* #1 bestseller, *Secrets of the Millionaire Mind*

"This is a game changer. Whether you are an executive, entrepreneur, investor, consultant, coach and/or mentor, this book is an absolute must read! This thought-provoking gem brings you the progressive business thinking of a Seth Godin, the personal development insights of a Tony Robbins, and the prodding for change of a Tom Peters. Don't just read this book. Reflect on the exceptional wisdom, and then adjust your actions to accelerate the success you so richly deserve."
—**Dave Carpenter,** success mentor to the stars

"Randy and I don't see eye-to-eye on some things, which is why this book freaks me out. Mainly because he's right. We've all been so busy learning how to not rock the boat; Randy shows us that we should be trying to flip it right over. Every area of business should take a real good look at what he says here or risk being capsized by people who have."

—**Scott Stratten**, author of *UnMarketing* and
The Book Of Business Awesome/UnAwesome

"As we've come to expect, Randy, in *Risky is the New Safe*, completely challenges our thinking and stretches our minds beyond traditional models and strategies and moves us to embrace the new world we live in with a passion for change and innovation that will give us the competitive advantage we need to succeed!"

—**Chris Widener**, founder, TwelveCoaches.com

"Randy Gage just made me miss a meeting. I was going to read the first few pages of his new book *Risky is the New Safe*, then go meet with my accountant. But I got hooked. I couldn't stop. The pages and the time flew by and I missed my meeting. (Sorry, James.) Damn I love this book. Kiss your assumptions about the future goodbye and be open to possibilities you never imagined. Do something risky. Read this book."

—**Joe Calloway**, author of *Becoming a Category of One*

"I think I held my breath through the entire first chapter. Randy paints a vivid picture of an exhilarating future if we heed his warnings and a terrifying one if we don't. Reading this book is the safest bet you've got."

—**Kyle Maynard**, two-time ESPY Award winner and
author of the *New York Times* bestseller *No Excuses*

"Once you read—and more importantly apply—the ideas contained in *Risky is the New Safe*, it will be impossible to go back to your old ways of thinking. Randy Gage will free your mind from the shackles of outdated thinking and give you tools that will enable you to navigate the greatest paradigm shift we are now in with the deftness of a Jedi Master. This is an outstanding work."

—**James Trapp**, President and CEO, Unity
Worldwide Ministries

"What would happen if John Naisbitt, George Orwell, and Ayn Rand co-authored a book? The result would be a glimpse of the future that is simultaneously inspiring, a little scary, and full of ideas about taking responsibility for your own success in an uncertain world. You no longer have to imagine. Randy Gage has written that book. *Risky is the New Safe* is a guide to prosperity in an age of uncertainty and chaos—a MUST read."
 —**Randy G. Pennington**, author of *Results Rule!*

"Thought provoking, even controversial in parts, this powerful book will have you re-thinking everything. Required reading for entrepreneurs and risk takers."
 —**Robert Ringer**, author of *The Entrepreneur: The Way Back for the U.S. Economy*

"Once again Randy Gage is two steps ahead of everyone else. This book is a blueprint for how to succeed in a new world that only leaders like Gage seem to understand. I couldn't put it down."
 —**Steve Siebold**, author of *Sex-Politics-Religion: How Delusional Thinking Is Destroying America*

"This is the book that should be compulsory reading for every employee, entrepreneur, business school, and university. Randy shares revolutionary truths and strategies for the new rules in sales, marketing, and harnessing the future of business."
 —**Frank Furness**, author of *Walking with Tigers—Success Secrets of the World's Top Business Leaders*

"This book doesn't just shift the way you will view the world. It will challenge everything you know about how to succeed! *Risky is the New Safe* is an astonishing read that will leave you excited, inspired, and well on your way to transformation. Buy this book right now!"
 —**Dan Thurmon**, author of *Off Balance on Purpose: Embrace Uncertainty and Create a Life You Love*

"You and I were trained to succeed in a world that no longer exists. Read that again. We have cultivated the skills that used to be needed. Now it's time to re-think . . . everything. Let Randy Gage be your guide into this exciting and somewhat disturbing new world that surrounds us. If you and I don't evolve again then we will surely become even more obsolete. Take the small *risk* of buying this book and reading it cover to cover. It's one of the *safest* things you can do."

—**Jim Cathcart**, author of *Relationship Selling and The Acorn Principle*

"I almost ran out of aspirin reading Randy's new book—it made my head hurt that much! But, it hurts for all the RIGHT reasons: he completely challenged my thinking and helped me see business in a fresh perspective. A friend of mine says, 'Those who are too afraid to make a mistake report to those who aren't.' Don't make the mistake of not reading this important business book—it's a gem."

—**Lou Heckler**, keynote business speaker, speaker coach, "Nightly Business Report" essayist on PBS television

"I love this book, and I love the thinking behind it even more. Once again Randy has pushed the button on what people accept as 'truth' and shows it to be false. The learning model of 'Better safe than sorry' leaves no one safe, and millions sorry. This book explains why; it's a must read."

—**Paul Martinelli**, international speaker, coach, and mentor

"When Randy Gage has something to say, you better listen. In this book he shares the secrets that will make you a success. The biggest risk you could take today would be to not read this book."

—**Shep Hyken**, *New York Times* bestselling author of *The Amazement Revolution*

"A really great book, *Risky is the New Safe* serves to help expand your current perspective of what the future might look like. You don't have to agree with everything, but the contrast can ignite your imagination in a fresh, wonderful, and inspiring way. It made me laugh, it made me question a few things, and it got me thinking . . . what if? Love that!"

—**Terri L. Sjodin**, principal and founder, Sjodin Communications, and bestselling author of *Small Message, Big Impact*

"Whether you like it or not, the world is changing. Whether you like him or not, Randy Gage can show you how to anticipate opportunities and prosper in a rapidly evolving world. His views are sometimes unorthodox, typically unconventional, and always unbeatable and that's exactly why you need to listen to him."

—**Rory Vaden**, co-founder Southwestern Consulting, *New York Times* bestselling author of *Take the Stairs*

"Gage does it again . . . turning everything you think you know upside down. His cutting edge look into the future, by shifting your paradigm today, will keep you surfing the wave of success!"

—**Louis Lautman**, director, *The Y.E.S. Movie* (www.theYESmovie.com)

"Brilliant, sardonic, funny, and forward thinking. Reading *Risky is the New Safe* is like sticking your finger in a light socket. Get a "shock to the future" . . . if you can handle it. The book takes life as you know it and jumps you into light speed. You may not like what you see, but boy, the ride is fun and it is worth taking a look. Strap in."

—**Victoria Labalme**, creative director, Labalme Communications

"At his brash take-no-prisoners best, Gage explores and exposes in fascinating detail today's number one Formula for Failure—Follow the Crowd—and then solidly sets his readers on the highroad speeding away to a future of positive and prosperous possibilities. Randy Gage is a genius. This book proves it."

—**John Milton Fogg**, author of *The Greatest Networker in the World*

"*Risky is the New Safe* is more than a book. It is a survival guide for an increasingly unpredictable future."

—**Joachim de Posada**, author of *Don't Eat the Marshmallow . . . Yet!*

"I divide learning into two categories: Direct Learning and Collision Learning. Direct learning is when someone says 'X' to you and 'X' is valuable. Collision Learning is when someone says 'X' to you, 'X' makes you think of 'Y' and 'Y' is valuable to you. Randy's book offers HUGE opportunities for both forms of learning (which is rare) on topics that are absolutely critical at this point in history. I recommend it highly."

—**Robert Scheinfeld**, *New York Times* bestselling author of *Busting Loose from the Money Game, The Ultimate Key to Happiness*, and other radically different multimedia resources for transformation

"If you haven't read a book lately that made you uncomfortable, you're playing it too safe. Read this book to stretch your thinking and improve your odds of success. The ideas you'll find here are edgy for the right reason: they'll get you to take the kind of intelligent risks and positive actions you very much need to succeed."

—**Mark Sanborn**, author of *The Encore Effect* and *Up, Down, or Sideways*

"*Risky is the New Safe* has me excited and I DO NOT excite easily! It paints a clear picture of what is, and an even clearer picture of what will be. This is the book that helps us move from change victims to change makers. If you're planning to live in this world a while longer—this book is not just your survival guide; it's your guide to surviving well."

—**Steve Keating**, consultant and professional speaker

"Randy Gage has a reputation for pulling no punches in calling it like it is. What he shares in *Risky is the New Safe* isn't to make you feel comfortable; it's to get you to act

and succeed. Consider it your new rulebook in these changing times."
—**Ric Thompson**, co-founder, HealthyWealthynWise.com

"No wonder there is so much advance buzz on this book! It's brilliant, will certainly be controversial to some, but real food for thought for critical thinkers. You may agree, you may disagree, but you have to read it."
—**Ford Saeks**, author of *Superpower: How to Think, Act, and Perform with Less Effort and Better Results*

"Randy Gage once again challenges your thoughts and beliefs—for your own good. If you are looking to rise up and take on life's challenges and create freedom, then *Risky is the New Safe* is required reading. The ROI from this book is insane! Bottom line: Buy it, read it, and then read it again."
—**JB Glossinger**, founder of MorningCoach.com
(#1 Rated Self-Help Podcast on iTunes)

"You know what they say about the opera? 'You'll laugh, you'll cry, you'll experience all human emotion.' Randy Gage's latest book is a lot like that. You'll laugh, you'll cry, you'll cheer, and you'll curse. But most of all, you'll think . . . a lot. After you barrel through the book the first time, go back and read it slowly and carefully, with a highlighter and a pen. When you're done, you'll find you've started writing the plan for the rest of your life."
—**Bruce Turkel**, brand expert and author
of *Building Brand Value*

"Talk about Future Shock! Forget *Who Moved my Cheese*—your whole LIFE is about to get a seismic shock. Randy paints a graphic picture about what's coming down the road—how to protect yourself and also how to benefit from it big time. Totally readable, utterly absorbing, *Risky is the New Safe* tells you what to do . . . and when to do it in order to protect, survive, and prosper in the coming years."
—**Stuart Goldsmith**, author of *The Midas Method, 7 Secrets of the Millionaires*, and other titles

"Gage is a genius! His brilliant ability to challenge you with hard truths makes you rethink almost everything. I'm buying the first 100 copies hot off the press for my business clients and team members!"

—**Lisa Jimenez**, MEd, author of *Conquer Fear!* and *Dont Mess with the Princess!*

"Risky is the New Safe is a thought-provoking, mind-expanding journey to your next adventure. Randy Gage's advice will guide you along a fresh path with no rules and encourage you to seek out new challenges. Especially if you consider yourself successful in life, you'd better pick up this book and read it now, because what was effective in the past won't work in the future."

—**Laura Stack**, author of *What to Do When There's Too Much to Do*, and 2011–2012 president, National Speakers Association

"This book is pure genius. I love it. You won't just get a glimpse of the future . . . it will hit you like a fire hose! And within a few pages, you'll realize that if you don't embrace the change NOW, you'll be left behind. Randy exposes the blatant transformation that is occurring right in front of our eyes . . . yet most are blind to it. These are game-changing trends that you must pay attention to."

—**Jordan Adler**, author of *Beach Money*

"If you're trying to decide if you should take a chance on buying this book, you're exactly the person who needs to read it! Twenty years from now people will look back and ask: How did Randy know all this was going to happen?"

—**Richard Fenton** and **Andrea Waltz,** authors of *Go for No!*®

"Riveting and exhilarating, *Risky is the New Safe* wakes you up with an ice-cold shower of disillusionment followed by a revitalizing bath of possibilities. Randy Gage shows how the rules have changed, and how you can win by daring to be different. Speaking especially to the entrepreneurial spirit, this book prepares us for what may turn out to be the most exciting time in human history."

—**Dr. Josephine Gross**, editor-in-chief, *Networking Times*

"Randy Gage has done it again. *Risky is the New Safe* will likely be another runaway bestseller. Why? Because it goes directly to the heart of how fast the rules of engagement are changing—head spinning fast. And for most of us these rules are like water to a fish . . . fairly invisible. Gage shines the spotlight on what we all need to do differently to win in this new game—both from a business and marketing viewpoint, to our own personal transformation."

—**Richard Bliss Brooke**, author of *Mach II with Your Hair on Fire: The Art of Vision & Self Motivation*

"Gage did it again! I was shocked, upset, entertained, captivated, and educated while reading this book. *Risky is the New Safe* made me evaluate my current strategy in business and in my life. Make sure that you buy, read and implement the teachings of this book. It is too risky not to."

—**Jeremiah Bradley**, co-CEO, Agel Enterprises

"This is a book for today . . . short, impactful, and strategic. These mind-changing concepts are designed to teach you how to be an effective entrepreneur in this brave new world."

—**Mark Yarnell**, bestselling author of 11 books on business, personal development, and network marketing

"Good books make you think. Great books make you think differently. Amazing books make you think in creative and innovative ways for success. Changing your thinking about what is 'safe' and what is 'risky' today is imperative for success. This book will show you the tools—and the right way to think—to succeed in this turbulent, completely different world. Get it and devour it!"

—**Terry Brock**, author of *Moving From Thinking "No Way" to "Net Yet!"*

"The first think you'll notice in *Risky is the New Safe* is that Gage doesn't tell you what to do. If that annoys you, you've identified the greatest challenge to your success. Randy's doing something far more

important . . . provoking you and me to think differently in order to reveal the possibilities that have been lying in wait since before our first breath. The irony is we were closer to those possibilities as infants than we are now as adults. If you let it, this book will give you the courage to claim what is yours."
—**Ian Percy**, innovation and possibilities expert

"This is a manifesto—a global warning—against the status quo. When Randy Gage rails against the machine, you better listen . . . carefully."
—**Mark Schaefer**, author of *Return On Influence* and
The Tao of Twitter

"Move over Darwin: *Risky is the New Safe* is the new survival guide for humans. Read it, use it."
—**Rebel Brown**, author of *Defy Gravity*

"I now have *Risky is the New Safe* painted on my office wall! I want my team reminded daily of the principles in this book. Couldn't buy just one—had to get a copy for my staff. You'll do the same!"
—**Chad Hymas**, author of *Doing
What Must Be Done*

"Randy Gage hits another one out of the park with this book! If you are tired of the daily grind and are looking for something different, this is the one to read. Randy will challenge your beliefs, your thoughts, and most importantly, the way you look at life. As he says in the book, 'When everyone is zigging, you want to be zagging,' and this book will show you how to do just that. Get it now!"
—**Stephanie Frank**, bestselling author
of *The Accidental Millionaire*

"If you are unprepared for an unpredictable future, you cannot blame Randy Gage. *Risky is the New Safe* should scare you away from 'safe' forever. More important, you now have the tools to find comfort and joy in 'risk.' The mistake would be taking all Gage says at 'face value.' Don't simply repeat his advice in the mirror or at

meetings. His message is deeper than his words. Think and prosper in the face of change and challenge."
—**David Yoho, Jr.**, president, Professional Educators Inc.

"Randy's latest work will kick your butt, freak you out, challenge your conventional beliefs, and likely make you uncomfortable . . . AND once you read the first page, you won't be able to put it down. Get ready to radically expand your thinking and gain perspective that ensures you don't just survive the big changes to come . . . you have the tools to THRIVE and can create prosperity in any economic climate."
—**Sonia Stringer**, author of *6 Steps to Six Figures and a Lifestyle You Love: The Ultimate Business-Building Guide for Women in Network Marketing*

"Randy Gage is much more than a teacher and a life coach. He is a Soul Coach and this book is a brilliant game plan for creating success."
—**Dale Ledbetter**, coauthor of *How Wall Street Rips You Off—And What You Can Do to Defend Yourself*

"You will be scared, provoked, and, if you read the entire book, encouraged by Randy Gage's new work, *Risky is the New Safe*. Randy describes the new landscape that your future will be built on . . . if you are willing to see it."
—**Barry Banther**, author and Fortune 500 management consultant

"In this book, Randy entreats us all to be contrarian. He pokes and prods our beliefs, making us look at how we run our lives—and the results we've achieved (or not) with those beliefs. You may get angry while reading this. That is a good thing as it's shaking up what you think is possible. Buy this book now to accelerate your progress."
—**Rebecca Morgan**, international management consultant and bestselling author of 25 books, including *Calming Upset Customers*

"I wouldn't say that *Risky is the New Safe* is a good book, or even a great one. It is a manifesto of individual and

global magnificence—a rare, seminal read. Ignore this instant classic at your own peril and that of those who matter to you."
— **Tim Durkin**, author of *Moving from PROMISE to PERFORMANCE: 17 Sure-Fire Strategies for Better Results at Work and Home*

"Our prayer is that all politicians would read this book! Since we already know all politicians won't read it, YOU really have to read it, because it gives you the insight to why we have all the problems we have today and how you can be pro-active and still enjoy getting rich. We will also give you a warning before you dig into it, because a few of Randy's examples are crossing the line of what we think should be in print. But when that is said, Randy's message is profound and is what all of us need to become leaders in this new economy."
— **Finn Orjan Saele** and **Hilde Rismyhr Saele,** co-founders, Zinzino AB, Scandinavia

"There couldn't have been a better book to talk about the new safe and the new normal for those seeking prosperity than *Risky is the New Safe;* and there couldn't have been a better (and more fun!) person to write about it than Randy Gage . . . characteristically contrarian, at times controversial, and all the time real . . . This is for those who dare to step out of the discomfort of their comfort and dare to be part of the new world order, where opportunities and prosperity abound like no other. It's risky, just the way we like it!"
— **Donna Imson**, executive chairperson, QNet Ltd, Hong Kong

"Fasten your seatbelts, Randy Gage takes you boldly where you've never gone before. At warp speed he brilliantly explores disruptive technology, cloning, free markets, the ego, prosperity, and cataclysmic change. He brings it all together and shows the kind of critical thinking required for success, and why playing it safe is the greatest risk of all."
— **Kathy Zader**, president, Zoom Strategies, Inc.

"In this new world economy where there is more complexity, more uncertainty, but also more opportunity than ever before, you need Randy Gage. This book is required reading for winning on the new economic playing field."
—**Patrick Stinus**, co-founder, Seventh Element LLC

"In this thought-provoking book, Randy Gage brilliantly illuminates the path for entrepreneurs who are open to new ways of thinking about prosperity and success."
—**Gina Carr**, MBA, CEO, Gina Carr International

"Just like the genie, Gage is out of the bottle with his focused road map for embracing the future. *Risky is the New Safe* offers transformative perspective with a shot of inspiration. It will help you get out of the safety zone, embrace risk, and move ahead of the future."
—**Ruby Newell-Legner**, CSP, author of 7 *Star Service Culture*
—*Turn Every Customer into a Fan*

RISKY
is the new
SAFE

The Rules
Have CHANGED...

A ROCK OPERA BY
RANDY GAGE

WILEY

John Wiley & Sons, Inc.

Published by John Wiley & Sons, Inc., Hoboken, New Jersey.
Published simultaneously in Canada.

For general information on our other products and services or for technical support, please contact our Customer Care Department within the United States at (800) 762-2974, outside the United States at (317) 572-3993 or fax (317) 572-4002.

Wiley publishes in a variety of print and electronic formats and by print-on-demand. Some material included with standard print versions of this book may not be included in e-books or in print-on-demand. If this book refers to media such as a CD or DVD that is not included in the version you purchased, you may download this material at http://booksupport.wiley.com. For more information about Wiley products, visit www.wiley.com.

Library of Congress Cataloging-in-Publication Data:

Gage, Randy.
    Risky is the new safe : the rules have changed : a rock opera / by Randy Gage.
       p. cm.
    ISBN 978-1-118-48147-9 (cloth); ISBN 978-1-118-50854-1 (ebk);
    ISBN 978-1-118-50856-5 (ebk); ISBN 978-1-118-50857-2 (ebk)
       1. Risk.   2. Success in business.   I. Title.
    HB615.G34 2013
    658.15′5—dc23

                                                                2012030211

Printed in the United States of America

10 9 8 7 6 5 4 3 2 1

*To Charles "Chuck" Dima, who taught me how
to win at softball . . . and life.
RIP, Coach.*

Contents

Acknowledgments   *xxi*

Synopsis: Safe Is the New Risky   *xxiii*

Overture   Training Monkeys and
                    Cloning Puppies   1

Act I   It's Not About the Tech   13

Act II   The Only Free Cheese Is
                    in the Mousetrap   29

Tenor Aria   The New Religion of Ideas   49

Act III   Move Fast and Break Things   63

Act IV   Harnessing the Ego for Success   95

Soprano Aria   Selfishness Is the New
                    Altruism   119

The After Party Sameness Creates Comfort;
                    Difference Creates Opportunity   133

Required Reading for Risk Takers   *141*

Connect with Randy!   *143*

Mad Love To . . .

My brilliant mastermind friends who reviewed early chapters and provided insights: Bob Burg, Dan Burrus, Terry Brock, Joe Calloway, Gina Carr, Joachim de Posada, Lisa Jimenez, Art Jonak, John David Mann, Ian Percy, Nido Qubein, Scott Stratten, Patrick Stinus, and Kathy Zader.

My copyeditor, the amazing Vicki McCown.

The lovely and talented John Wiley & Sons team, led by Matt Holt, with Adrianna Johnson, Christine Moore, and Peter Knox.

And my very own version of Pepper Potts: Lornette Browne.

You guys are the best!

Synopsis
Safe Is the New Risky

A Rock Opera in Four Acts

Overture: Training Monkeys and Cloning Puppies

Human workers are now being replaced with monkeys and cloning is fast becoming a reality. The old economic model is broken. Huge, household-name companies that play it safe will vanish, and emerging, upstart companies willing to take risks will prevail.

Act I: It's Not about the Tech

Mobile apps, the cloud, and disruptive technology are eliminating millions of jobs, but they will also create remarkable new opportunities. What happens when virtual reality sex and holo-suites become a reality?

Act II: The Only Free Cheese Is in the Mousetrap

Class warfare creates a dictatorship and entitlement programs enslave the masses. The best ways to protect yourself when the euro collapses and governments go bankrupt.

Tenor Aria: The New Religion of Ideas

The West is getting lazy and there is potential for a new world order. In the new economy, ideas will become the most valuable currency.

Act III: Move Fast and Break Things

Marketing is dead; social media is alive. Pharmaceuticals are out; tofu burgers are in. Retail is cold; multi-level marketing is hot. Contrarians will win the day when down is up and up is down.

Act IV: Harnessing the Ego for Success

How genius entrepreneurs harness and channel their ego for results. A look at the high-level achievers Napoleon Hill studied, as well as the new billionaires of today, reveals they have strong egos.

Soprano Aria: Selfishness Is the New Altruism

Can selfishness really be a virtue? How people—and companies—make the journey from self-consciousness to cosmic consciousness.

The After Party: Sameness Creates Comfort; Difference Creates Opportunity

If you ask the wrong question, the answer doesn't matter. Dare to risk—because in the new world, risky is the new safe.

RISKY
is the new
SAFE

Overture

Training Monkeys and Cloning Puppies

I was at an eco-preserve outside of Phuket, Thailand, when suddenly I realized that the world had changed forever.

The reason for my visit was to cross another item off my bucket list: riding an elephant through the rainforest. There was a wait for the elephants, so they asked if I wanted to see the monkey-training show.

Monkey training? Who could resist, I thought.

But these monkeys weren't being trained to dance to organ music or perform parlor tricks. They were being taught to harvest coconuts. *In place of people*. It was quite fascinating, really. Each tree had a wire running from the ground to the top of the tree. The monkeys climbed the wire to the treetop, where they hung on with one hand and one foot. With their other hand and foot, they spun each coconut round and round until it fell to the ground.

It costs about US$300 and takes a couple months to get your monkey trained. Once trained, the average monkey will harvest 1,000 coconuts a day!

Coming home from the same trip, I overnighted in San Francisco to break up the travel. In the airline lounge the next morning, I noticed a couple who had a cute little puppy peeking out of a travel carrier. Since I love all animals, I asked if I could play with him. They agreed and said something quite shocking:

"Our puppy is a clone."

Of course I thought they were joking. They weren't. They informed me that they were returning from South Korea where they had picked up the dog after it had been cloned from the DNA cells of their beloved family pet who had died.

I was about as skeptical as anyone could be. This frisky puppy with bright eyes was as adorable as any dog you've ever seen.

The couple and their puppy were on my flight home to Miami, where the husband took the dog to the economy cabin several times to show it to people back there. I was intrigued but still doubtful, until we arrived at Miami International Airport. There was a phalanx of reporters and camera crews milling around the baggage carousels, all waiting to greet the guest of honor.

The puppy's picture was on the front page of the *Miami Herald* the next day, along with the story of his cloning. Turns out he wasn't the first puppy ever cloned, just the first to come to the United States. And, of course, sheep and camels and other animals have been cloned as well.

Recently Oxitec, a British biotech company, created an uproar in Key West, Florida, with their proposal to eradicate the Dengue virus by introducing a genetically modified mosquito. Within a few weeks, a petition against the idea collected 100,000 signatures, with people expressing fear about "Robo-Frankenstein" and "mutant" mosquitoes.

How long will it be before someone else is proposing a genetically modified wolf, shark, or other animal to correct a population imbalance, spread of disease, or other ecosystem problem—which is probably the result of man changing the natural order to begin with?

And then, when someone starts offering genetically modified humans, things really get fascinating . . .

You think abortion creates controversy now, wait until this science evolves. Will parents decide on abortions because their tyke is going to have brown eyes instead of blue? How much will prospective mothers pay to ensure their newborn child has no congenital disorders, no hereditary diseases, and Maya Angelou's poetry gene? How much will prospective fathers pay to ensure their newborn son has enough athletic ability to start in the NFL or NBA?

You can debate the ethics of this and hate it like a poison—but it is coming soon. And someone will make enough money with this to fill the Grand Canyon.

We'll likely be debating the ethical and moral dilemmas of genetic modification and cloning for years— but the genie isn't going back in the bottle.

All the Rules Have Changed . . .

When I was growing up, my mom told me to go to school, earn a degree, and get a job with a big company— then, I would be set for life. That was the safe thing to do, and millions of other parents around the world were telling their children to do the same thing.

Today, however, that might be the riskiest thing you can do . . .

Fortunately, I was expelled from high school, so I never got a chance to follow my mother's advice. And *not* following that safe path has made me a very rich man.

If you work in the corporate world today, you have a target on your back. And the longer you've worked for a company, the bigger that target is. Long gone are the days when an employee's longevity at a job was a guarantee for security and a company's loyalty. Companies today often see long-term employees as liabilities. They want to figure out whether they can turn an employee into a contractor or replace them with someone younger who works cheaper, has less accrued vacation time, and receives fewer benefits—or better yet, maybe they can outsource that job overseas and pay even less.

Imagine an executive at American Airlines seeing that monkey training show in Thailand. Can't you just picture him thinking, "Hmm . . . I wonder if we could replace our flight attendants with monkeys?"

Obviously I'm joking, as flight attendants play an important role in maintaining passenger safety. (And I'm writing this from seat 5G of an American 777 right now.) But make no mistake: There are millions of jobs that can and probably someday *will* be performed by monkeys—or dogs or cats or dolphins. Think about it: We've been using camels, horses, and mules as beasts of burden for centuries, so training animals to perform more sophisticated jobs is a logical next step. As new developments expand the number of species with which this is possible, chaos in the workforce will ensue.

Oh, there will always be jobs for humans. But there will be far fewer of them, and they'll be quite different from the ones we have now. Some of them will be designing the robots that will replace the humans in their jobs. Some of them will be working at the animal training farms. And some of them will be at the animal cloning farms. *Oh, and some will be at the human cloning farms . . .*

Why will Jones & Sons Hardware on Main Street need to hire any outside employees when Mr. Jones, Sr., can clone all the boys he needs? Why keep paying average employees if you can clone six more of your best one? Why give tenure to a college professor when you can roll a brand new one off the assembly line whenever you need one?

These developments will create a sea change in every sector of every industry in the world—and every sector of every industry off-world as well. Everything you now know as safe is about to become very risky.

I See Dead People

Look around you everywhere. What do you see? Millions of lifeless zombies drifting through lives of quiet desperation. These people are dead, but they don't have enough sense to lie down. They think *The Matrix* was a science fiction film, when actually they're living (or undead) proof that it was actually a documentary.

They work in dead, lifeless companies that have shrinking market share and declining profits, which they attribute to increased competition, a tough economy, or variables like rising price of materials. But those things are the symptoms, not the cause.

These companies lack a pulse because they're operating in an economic model that was designed for another time. The model they follow was built when goods were produced in Europe and traveled by ship to the New

World, where they were transported by stagecoach to population centers and sold in general stores. And even though stagecoaches gave way to trains or trucks, and general stores evolved into shopping malls, the basic system never changed. But the world did.

Developments like fax machines, overnight shipping, and toll-free numbers, and now mobile phones, the Internet, and social media have altered everything about the way we do business.

But no one noticed the target had moved . . .

People continued to elect representatives or follow benevolent dictators, confident that government would provide security and take care of their needs. They spent years of their lives and went into debt to the tune of tens of thousands of dollars to get diplomas that are no longer viable in the employment world. They kept pledging their loyalty to corporations, thinking that would provide for retirement security, because that's what their parents had done. And once they went to work for those dead, lifeless corporations, they were indoctrinated with the same mind viruses as the old-timers working there.

Airlines kept doing hub-and-spoke operations because they had always done it that way. TV networks broadcasted by satellite to affiliates and sold commercials because that's how it was always done. Travel agencies opened more offices; video chains kept stocking DVD stores; and newspapers continued to print large sheets of paper with day-old news. Retailers continued the system of warehouses, rack-jobbers, distributors, and stores because they were invested in it. Some of those retailers even built large spaces to sell nostalgic, novelty items (you're holding one now), which, in the not-so-distant future, half of the potential market will only have seen in a museum.

Playing It Safe Is the Biggest Risk

Everybody is playing it safe, because they think that's the smart thing to do. But in today's new economy, playing it safe is the *riskiest* thing you can do.

All the rules have changed and they're going to change more tomorrow. Disruptive technology, changing cultural trends, a breakdown of the education system, government corruption and malfeasance, and a society that is in some ways evolving—and in other ways devolving—has moved the target. And it keeps moving, faster every day.

Millions of people have been assimilated by the Borg and wander aimlessly through life as worker drones in the collective. And the companies run and staffed by all these people are facing extinction because they can't compete in the new world. If the definition of insanity really is doing the same thing over and over and expecting a different result, these people and companies are stark, raving mad.

It's not unlike the analogy that Dr. Ken Dychtwald (a brilliant guy, by the way) uses when he relates how companies reacted to the age wave caused by the millions of baby boomers. He paints the picture of a huge elephant migrating across the decades. Most companies are desperately chasing after the elephant, shooting arrows in its butt. What they really need to do is get in front of the elephant and dig a big hole.

The people who create prosperity in the new economy will be in front of the trends, anticipating them instead of naively reacting to what happened yesterday.

It doesn't matter whether you're an individual or a company. To create wealth or success today, you have to become a critical thinker and blow up conventional wisdom. Because not only is the current economic model not working well; it's actually moving toward a serious breakdown.

I'm not a futurist, but I'll make a few predictions . . .

Hundreds of millions more jobs will be eliminated by technology, or will require complete retraining or certification for workers to continue doing them. Complete industries will disappear. State-sponsored education will be unable to remain relevant. The euro (and perhaps some other currencies) will collapse within the next two to three years. Tens of thousands of companies will go bankrupt, as will some countries.

Ain't It Great! Here's the Really Good News . . .

Every challenge creates a corresponding opportunity. Some of the greatest wealth was created during the Great Depression—just as many fortunes are created in every recession.

When everyone is zigging, you want to be zagging.

At the exact moment you're reading this sentence, you're living in the greatest time in human history. There has never been a better time to be alive. The speed and scope of changes taking place in the world (and solar system) today offer unprecedented opportunities for living a life of prosperity.

Advances in science, medicine, and nutrition will offer breakthroughs in longevity, health, and wellness. Technology will create new business models and recreate old ones, offering extraordinary avenues for creating wealth. And all this development will provide you with yet more ways to live a life of meaning, growth, and adventure.

During their lifetime, the vast majority of people who read this book will have the opportunity to vacation on the moon, buy a condo on the ocean floor with a spectacular coral-reef view, or take a feed from the midfielder and score the goal that wins the World Cup for their country. (Although this last one will probably be done via virtual reality in a holo-suite.) This is the fascinating world we will explore together.

If you are willing to take risks and become a contrarian, there are—and will continue to be—extraordinary opportunities for success and prosperity. Because in the new economy, risky is the new safe . . .

Act I

It's Not About the Tech

Anyone who fights for the Future lives in it today.
                    —Ayn Rand, *The Romantic Manifesto*

Be nice to that impudent teenage store clerk who's playing *Angry Birds* on his iPhone instead of paying attention to you. Chances are good you'll be working for him one day.

We could talk about travel agents, video store clerks, and the millions of other jobs that have been eliminated by technology and won't be replaced. But that's so 2012 . . .

The real disruptions caused by technology are only just beginning.

If you're a parent who wants to help your 14-year-old son or daughter plan for the future, you're about to tackle a difficult feat. Because the best jobs of 2018 haven't even been invented yet. But we do know one thing for sure: Taking the safe path won't get you there.

We are entering an era of technological advances so profound it will be breathtaking. And the opportunities this era brings will be just as breathtaking, because wealth is the product of humankind's capacity to innovate.

The major factors driving these opportunities are:

- The explosion of smartphones and tablets
- An abundance of bandwidth
- The attention-deficit-disorder generation coming of age

- Advances in video resolution
- The elimination of division between broadcast, cable, and Internet content providers
- The love affair between people and mobile apps

Let's start with television: The average person in the developed world now watches five to six hours of television a day. But what we're talking about is bigger than TV.

We can look at the Internet as an example as well. Probably nothing has changed the world more in the past century than the web. But the change on the horizon is bigger than the Internet. What we're really talking about isn't the technology itself, but how people use that technology. Two-screen viewing, using a TV and tablet or smartphone together, is increasing rapidly. This creates many new possibilities for interaction, and where it will end up remains to be seen.

We're now entering the third wave of tech companies. Wave one was the portals like AOL, Yahoo!, and Google. They attracted us by helping to make sense of the web by organizing and aggregating it into categories we could understand and access. The next generation was the social web, an area in which probably no one has done better than Facebook. But Facebook will become the new MySpace, if they don't morph quickly into mobile. The big winners in the third generation will be the companies that figure out how to monetize mobile.

This is why Facebook recently shelled out a billion dollars to buy Instagram, a photo-sharing program that allows users to digitally filter their photos and share them via a number of social networking services.

So yes, we're talking about mobile and the cloud, but this change is bigger than even that. Mobile transformed the Internet, and the cloud will transform both to mind-boggling degrees. (Cloud computing is digital file storage as a service, hosting a user's data on an external network allowing them access from their own devices.)

Things are moving at breathtaking speed from the Internet to mobile apps. In the very near future, if you were to force a person to choose between giving up their favorite apps versus their favorite websites, they will likely keep their apps. Meanwhile, broadcast networks are trying to figure out how to compete with cable; cable networks are trying to figure out how to compete with the Internet; websites are trying to figure out how to offer themselves via mobile; and mobile sites are trying to figure out how to do apps. They're all like the wagon train under attack. They've circled the wagons, but they're all shooting inward.

This isn't about broadcast versus cable, or Apple TV. Consumers don't care about a company's turf wars. They just want to be informed and entertained. They want to sound like they know what they're talking about when the subjects of politics or their favorite sports team come up. And most desperately of all, they want to be distracted and entertained every waking moment of every day.

There is now a whole generation of people who are tethered electronically, 24 hours a day. Suggest to them that they should leave their cell phones at home when they go to the opera or church, and they'll look at you like you're eating spiders. The very concept is so alien to them they can't even process the request.

They'll argue something about how necessary their phone is in case of an emergency, disregarding the 5,000 years of human history we survived before the cell phone. The real reason that they need to take it everywhere is simply that they have become addicted to their electronic pacifier.

We are more connected than ever, yet we are lonelier than ever. The average person is bored to death, insecure, and can't stand to have a moment alone in quiet thought. People need to be BUSY all the time. So whether it means sending and checking text messages while eating dinner with their spouse, replying to emails while they're in line at the checkout counter, or watching cat videos during a red light, they want content—and an endless supply of it.

To Vid or Not to Vid

Now, this raises the issue about video. We are definitely a visual society nowadays, and we're becoming even more so. Radio continues to exist, but only in the shadow of television and movies. Pretty much everyone under the age of 35 is part of the Internet/texting/TV/video game generation. That's a nice way to say they have the attention span of a gnat.

You have to figure that video is the best way to capture their attention. My friend and bestselling author Brendon Burchard predicts that 95 percent of everything on the Internet, including email, will be video within a couple years. Now, Brendon's a clever fellow, so I'm inclined to agree with him, but as a critical thinker, I have to assume everything will be video—unless it isn't.

Personally, I hate getting video emails. The lighting is usually dreadful, they take too long to watch, and I can't start to reply to questions without stopping the video and having to replay it from the beginning. I'm old enough to remember a time—specifically, the fifth grade—when people talked about video telephones as though they were the stuff of science fiction. This was something you'd see on *The Jetsons*. Now we're in 2012, the technology has been available for years—and no one wants it.

Turns out that not all women want to answer a videophone when they have curlers in their hair. And most guys don't like to answer the videophone naked and wet from the shower. I usually do four or five Skype conferences a week, and about 90 percent of the time, they're done by audio, without the video. (Although little kids now use tablets to call each other, using apps like FaceTime. My friend's four-year-old talks with all her friends using her iPad, screen within a screen. With just a phone and no video they lose interest fast.)

So where will video end up in the equation? I don't know, and neither does anyone else, but the smart bet is that it will play a huge factor. And speaking of video, this takes us back to the issue of television, movies, and streaming Internet.

Seven Billion Channels and Everything's On

The question is not how many broadcast networks will survive or how many cable networks are offered in your local market. Soon there will be seven billion networks with seven billion programming directors. You and every other human on earth will program *The My Network (TMN)*.

You'll order new pilots, season-long episodes of dramas, sitcoms, reality and talk shows, sporting events, holiday specials, concert presentations, and more—just like network executives do now. The difference is that TMN will be customized exactly to your tastes; it will gather and provide content that's been designed uniquely for you from everywhere.

So your version of TMN might include: *The X Factor* (U.S. and U.K. editions); *CSI* (Miami, New York, and Lunar editions); *Game of Thrones*; Seth Godin's blog; Gary Vaynerchuk's Tumblr feed; Shane Dawson and Mystery Guitar Man's YouTube channels; the Twitter feeds from your "fave" list; all Manchester United matches; new releases from Maroon 5, the Fray, and Lady Gaga; your Empire Avenue stock price feeds; your E*TRADE real stock price feeds; all *Avengers* and *Star Trek* sequels; Sirius XM radio; breaking news updates from CNN; all the feeds from your Facebook friends and LinkedIn groups; the Pinterest boards on waterskiing and comic books; the electronic versions of the *Wall Street Journal* and *ESPN* the magazine; your iTunes playlist; this semester's classes from your online university; electronic discount coupons from any business you're about to walk or drive by; and, of course, all new books from me.

Migrating from Screen to Screen

The last thing you're going to care about is on which network or channel you can find all these options or even the screen for which they were first created. You'll want to watch your network on your smartphone or wristwatch when you're at the mall, on your tablet during lunch break, and on the screen in your car while you're driving home (I know, this should be illegal). Your network will automatically load to your eight-foot-wide HD TV when you walk into your living room, and spontaneously switch to your computer monitor when you sit down at your desk.

Of course, this trend will be short-lived and eventually die when Google perfects their eyeglasses. And the glasses will be short-lived and eventually die when someone else puts the technology in a contact lens. And there will obviously be a retro trend back to screens, when the attention-deficit generation discovers that they can't watch six different screens at the same time in their lens, the way they did on satellite TV.

This is not 20 or 30 years in the future we're talking about here, kids. These innovations will be part of our lives way before this decade is over.

The legacy networks still don't get this. Instead of NBC scouting YouTube to discover their next television star, they need to change their paradigm and discover the next multichannel star they can offer to TMN.

The process is starting now. Netflix is creating original content, cable networks are developing their own shows, and YouTube is grooming the stars on their own platform. But all those lines between networks, channels, and screens are going to disappear. Instead of promos like "Tonight, 8 p.m. Eastern on FOX," taglines will say, "Click here to get it *now*."

·   All of this will open up *amazing* possibilities for entrepreneurs. The cost of entry to become a show producer, publisher, or movie director will drop dramatically. You can buy an HD Flip video camera nowadays for $200, and it does the job that required a $75,000 camera 15 years ago. A movie like *Titanic*, which originally cost $100 million dollars to make, might be done for *$100,000* in 2018. (Provided you can get Leonardo and Kate to work for a percentage of the revenue.) Meantime, James Cameron will be making the remastered version for about $100 billion, which will be done in virtual reality, so you can feel the freezing water splash on you and smell the chicken in the dining room scene.

The financial possibilities for all content creators—whether audio, print, or video (and throw in sensory)—are going to be beyond stunning. In the same way that iTunes completely revolutionized the music business, these technologies will remake dozens of other businesses, from publishing to entertainment, education to marketing, medical care to manufacturing.

But Before You Catch Your Breath, Mobile Apps Will Change It All Again

Once again, this change won't be about the technology, the product, or the company offering it. *It will be about how consumers use the app to enhance their lives.*

The big boom in apps won't be the proprietary ones that companies create for their customers, although this will produce trillions of dollars in revenues. The biggest share will come from generic process apps—the ones that help you catch a cab, find a restaurant, locate a dance studio, check references on a dentist, rate a hotel, hook up for sex, and about 10 million other things I can't think of right now.

The US Airways app will tell you your gate and departure time. The process app will tell you the truth about how late it will take off. The Vito's Pizza app will allow you to order a medium pepperoni with extra cheese; but because it's compiled by actual customers, the process app will tell you if Vito washes his hands after using the bathroom.

Walmart is currently testing an iPhone-based, self-checkout system which allows you to scan your own purchases and pay without having to stop by a cash register. (For younger readers, "cash" was a form of paper and metal currency that people used to use in exchange for goods and services.)

Naturally, this app was pioneered by Apple, who is currently using it in many of their own stores. Customers browse a display of accessories, then scan and pay for what they want entirely through the app. They can enter, buy, and leave the store without ever interacting with a clerk.

Here's the really intriguing thing . . .

Most of this cataclysmic change is coming about because of the emergence of smartphones. What about all the other potential smart appliances?

For example, I just remodeled one of my bathrooms. I installed a new toilet that opens and starts playing music as you walk toward it, automatically flushes and closes the lid after you use it (obviously designed by a woman!), and has a built-in bidet, dryer, light, and radio. You control the light, radio, water temperature, and the angle and pressure of the water from an electronic track pad remote control. The manufacturer doesn't categorize it as a smart toilet, but I certainly would. How long before we have smart refrigerators that notice when you get down to your last three cans of Dr. Pepper and automatically reorder your next 12-pack? The people who facilitate that process with technology, inventory control, payments, and delivery will make fortunes. Imagine the possibilities of smart ovens, washer/dryers, and other appliances.

Gamification is exploding right now. Empire Avenue added a gaming aspect to social media, and it's gained a passionate following of devotees. (Like me.) Even some online dating sites are now adding games to the equation. People seem to love the social interaction, competition, and entertainment values of sites and mobile apps that offer this. Where will they end up? No one knows—and anyone who says they do is lying.

Now It Gets Real. Kind Of.

There is another development that may provide more sea changes in society than everything we've discussed so far: That's when virtual reality comes into its own.

As I mentioned earlier, most people today are bored to tears with their lives. They just want to be entertained. That's what will drive all the content we just looked at.

But when things get virtual, all bets are off . . .

Virtual life looks a lot more inviting than actual life. There are no enlarged prostates, traffic jams, or canceled flights in the virtual world. You'll never have to face rejection or ridicule, get fired, or lose a championship game. There are no chores to do, everyone likes you, and there's always a happy ending.

Now picture owning a holo-suite franchise (or better yet, offering the franchises) that provides people with a place to come after work where they can experience virtual-reality vacations, concerts, acting out their favorite movies or novels, climbing a mountain, defeating the Nazis (or the Klingons), playing guitar with Slash, singing a duet with Placido Domingo, hitting a home run off of Justin Verlander, dropping the bass like Skrillex at Ultra, blocking the shot from Lionel Messi, or drinking tea with Jesus.

Now, we're not talking about *watching* believable movies of these experiences. You will actually be able to take part in them as though you were there. You'll experience sight, taste, sound, smell, and touch; feel your heart race, the tingle of breeze on your neck, or the perspiration rolling down your back.

This industry will create trillions in income for developers, programmers, authors, graphic designers and animators, center owners, and their marketers. It will probably also create serious mental health issues for millions of people and generate great tension in millions of relationships, which, in turn, will generate more trillions of dollars for addiction centers, therapists, psychologists, marriage counselors, and drug companies. And we haven't even discussed the mother of all consumer products: sex.

Virtual Reality Sex

Consider all the sex toys available now, hook them up to manually pleasure whatever organs or orifices float your boat, augment with sensors all over your body, create your ideal script, and add the program that projects the perfect partner—either a specific movie star you choose, or your perfect match customized from a catalog of hair and eye color, facial features, and body parts.

You and your partner (or partners) will be as wild and kinky as you can possibly fantasize. (And for those of you with more discriminating tastes, you can opt for pedophilia, bestiality, or necrophilia—without the inconvenience of prison!)

You think guys today desert their families and spend their kids' college fund on a gambling junket to Vegas? What do you think they'll do when offered this option? This industry alone could cause a catastrophic breakdown in the family unit, long-term relationships, and the institution of marriage. (A societal change that will again offer trillions of dollars more for all those people, mentioned above, who help with that sort of thing.)

If the woman (and it will probably be a woman) who perfects virtual reality sex is able to protect the technology with a patent, she will become the richest human being on earth—at least until human cloning becomes accepted and some third-world nation starts producing sex-worker clones. Then, the virtual reality sex business craters overnight.

Remember: *When everyone else is zigging, you want to be zagging*.

You might be 50 or 60 years old and incredibly frightened by technology. I'm 53 and approached it kicking and screaming, so I feel your pain. But I don't think this computer fad is going to blow over.

That antisocial kid who tunes out the rest of the world to play video games all day will be uniquely qualified to pilot an asteroid-mining spaceship, program those virtual-reality vacation packages, or perform heart transplant surgery—which of course, he'll do remotely from the control room, using robotics and a joystick.

Mobile, social media, and apps are going to transform every aspect of our lives. You can't sit these out. And truth is, once you get over your fears, the technology is pretty simple to understand. And the way the technology is advancing, the risk continues to diminish. It becomes easier to use, is accepted earlier, and the cost keeps coming down.

No matter what business you are in—whether you're an international oil company or a movie studio, a neighborhood beauty salon or a chiropractor—technology is changing everything. It will impact the way you run your business, market it, and manage it. These new technologies will present many challenges for all companies; however, they'll also create very lucrative opportunities for those willing to take risks.

You want to be out *in front* of the charge. But you have to keep in mind that change isn't really about the technology itself: It's all about how people will use technology to solve problems and make their lives easier or more enjoyable. If you can figure that out, you'll become very wealthy indeed. And while you may think you need a crystal ball to do that, that's really not the case.

Here's the other really intriguing thing about the future: Most of it can actually be predicted with an amazing degree of accuracy.

Check out the book *Flash Foresight* by Daniel Burrus with John David Mann. It's an insightful look at the kinds of change we can look at to find certainty. Once you understand the difference between cyclic versus linear change and soft versus hard trends, predicting the future gets a whole lot easier—and a whole lot more lucrative.

Keep one thing in mind: It's not about the tech. It's about the few who figure out how people want to use that tech.

Act II

The Only Free Cheese Is in the Mousetrap

Whether you went to the original release of the movie *Titanic* back in 1998, to the 3-D version released in 2012, or will attend the virtual reality version in 2020, you're still going to know how it ends. The ship sinks and people die.

The ending is no less predictable when you look around the world today and see how governments manage their budgets and manipulate the economy. Economies are going to crash and people are going to get hurt.

Of course, many *other* people will become wealthy. These are the ones who embrace risk, welcome change, and get ahead of trends. Paradigms will shift, challenges will arise, and those who provide solutions will prosper as they always have.

True prosperity is always created by value-for-value exchanges. There will be a huge demand for people and companies that solve problems. But the old tactics that we considered to be safe—putting money in a savings account, buying government bonds, and relying on government-sponsored retirement programs—are the new risky.

Many governments today follow Keynesian economic theories. Though these are widely accepted, they simply don't work. These theories are based upon a philosophy that the state not only knows best how the marketplace works (which is simply ludicrous), but also that government can actually *benevolently control* an economy (which is beyond ludicrous, as illustrated by the disastrous results of current events). Hundreds of billions of transactions are completed every day, each by someone looking for what is best for them. To operate under a system that claims that a central government knows what's best for all is not only ridiculous—it's also dangerous.

These theories suggest that countries can spend more money than they take in, and if the deficit is scaled to a certain percentage of GDP, it doesn't matter. This is no different than the analysts who were hyping zero-revenue models during the dot-com bubble. The fact that everybody wanted to believe it was true didn't *make it true*.

The whole dot-com debacle and the economic policies that governments practice today are no less silly than the old joke, "We lose money on every sale, but we make it up in volume."

As I'm writing this, European Union governments are enduring a great deal of upheaval. People are demonstrating in Greece, and the countries that have done a better job managing their budgets are furious with the ones that did not. They're demanding these bankrupt countries slash more expenses to get their budgets in line. But, of course, the populations in those countries are rebelling. All across Europe, work slowdowns, strikes, and demonstrations are on the rise.

I strongly believe that the euro will collapse as a result of all this political unrest. At some point very soon, it will be untenable for politicians in some of these bankrupt countries to put in place the austerity that other member nations demand. The politicians in the *have* countries will find it equally indefensible to keep increasing taxes on their own citizens to subsidize the *have-not* countries. To do so would mean getting kicked out of office by the voters—something that's already happening as I type these words.

The concept behind the euro was flawed, and the way in which it was implemented didn't help matters. Instead of an actual fiscal union with centralized taxing and spending policies, the eurozone creators substituted rules on the size of member countries' debt and deficits. However, despite the fact that these rules were spelled out in the Maastricht Treaty, none of the member countries followed them—not even fiscally conservative Germany.

So How Does This Happen?

When the first *have* country opts out of the euro, it will have a domino effect, in which most of the viable countries no longer recognize or use the euro within a matter of months. (Or perhaps just a handful of the original member states keep the euro in place.) Most or all countries will go back to their old currencies—and when they do, they will take the opportunity to make up their budget shortfalls by devaluing the reintroduced pre-euro currencies. While this might provide short-term relief, it will ultimately make inflation worse, and cause horrendous long-term damage to each country. It will bring on a financial bloodbath that will affect the dollar, pound, yen, and all other currencies.

Many people will lose fortunes. But others will make them.
(More about that in a minute . . .)

We have set a mind-numbing record for budget deficits here in the United States. If a 2012 presidential candidate promised to actually balance the budget, he or she would be labeled an extremist lunatic and laughed out of the race. Why? Because the cuts required for the United States to live within its means would be so drastic they would incite rioting in the streets, and possibly a civil war.

A Line Has Been Crossed

In many places around the globe, we have crossed over a line that spells ominous trouble for the future.

The people who are receiving government assistance now outnumber the people who are producing and paying into the kitty. Government entitlement programs have run amok. And once you provide an entitlement for someone, they begin to see it as their right. We've lost sight of one of the basic tenets of our Constitution and Bill of Rights. To quote Thomas Jefferson:

> To take from one because it is thought that his own industry and that of his father's has acquired too much, in order to spare to others, who, or whose fathers, have not exercised equal industry and skill, is to violate arbitrarily the first principle of association—the guarantee to every one of a free exercise of his industry and the fruits acquired by it.

The government mismanagement of budgets and entitlement programs is wiping out wealth, hurting everyone—especially the poor—and driving a wedge between wealth classes.

It's quite probable the next Hitler won't be a racist, but instead a demagogue inciting the masses to overthrow or even kill the wealthy. And there are a lot of disenfranchised, frustrated people with entitlement and victim mentality who will buy into this quite readily.

As I was writing this chapter, I received something that I initially thought was an Internet prank, but incredulously wasn't: Katja Kipping, the leader of Germany's Socialist Left Party has called for a 100 percent tax on any income above €40,000 a month. Think about that for a minute: *100 percent!* Kipping's rationale is that "there's no additional life enjoyment, anyway" for those earning more than that. (As an aside, I do earn more than €40,000 a month, and I can assure you, there is more life enjoyment.) She admitted that she got the idea from French presidential candidate Jean-Luc Mélenchon, who demanded a 100 percent tax on any income above €360,000 year.

The problem with all this soak-the-rich philosophy is that it is in direct violation of the laws that govern prosperity. And ironically, the real victims of this philosophy are actually the poor. They're the last to get hired, the first to get laid off, the most in need of assistance, and the least likely to have the resources to deal with adversity.

Kipping is also proposing a basic stipend for all German citizens of €1,050 a month. Like most collectivists, she discounts the most important thing: Governments can give something to one person only by taking it from another. Introducing these types of onerous taxes only causes productive citizens to flee to other countries. You drive out the best producers and, once again, actually hurt the poor the most.

Some of these economic theories would have you believe that governments get to operate by a different set of rules than the rest of us—but they don't. The prosperity principles for governments are no different than they are for people.

The Only Free Cheese Is in the Mousetrap

So how did we get here? And what do we do about it? We must first recognize the cause of all this crazy dysfunctional economic theory. No matter how many political parties democracies and republics begin with, they inevitably evolve into two-party systems. The evolution process causes the two parties that remain standing to be diametrically opposed to each other in their philosophical positions. During this evolution, parties with similar philosophies are integrated into the two that survive the cut.

While the names might be different in different countries, those labels are meaningless. One party will be liberal and the other conservative. More importantly, one party will be in power and one party will be out of power. And power corrupts even some of the most idealistic, well-meaning people (not to mention a lot of cynical, ill-meaning ones).

The party in power wants to remain in power, and the party out of power wants to get back into power.

And the only way to do that is by getting more votes than the other party. *And the best way to do that is to give free cheese.*

Let's say, for example, Party A offers free prescriptions. Party B sees the bet and raises it to free health care. Party A raises the ante with student loans. Party B comes back with free education.

Now everybody wants the cheese, but nobody wants to pay for it. The politicians need a majority to get elected, and there are more people who have a little bit of cheese (or none at all) than there are people with lots of cheese. So the platform evolves to taxing the productive people more to subsidize the nonproductive. The message becomes populist:

"The rich can afford more."

"Everyone needs to pay their fair share."

"The needs of the many outweigh those of the few."

The population is already infected with dozens of mind viruses that pop culture, organized religion, and governments have brainwashed into them. Some of the most prevalent ones are:

- Money is bad.
- Rich people are evil.
- It's spiritual (or noble) to be poor.
- You have to sell your soul for money.
- Money doesn't buy happiness.
- Big companies get rich by exploiting poor people and plundering all the natural resources.

One of my earlier books, *Why You're DUMB, SICK and BROKE and How to Get SMART, HEALTHY and*

RICH! explores the issues of programming and mind viruses in greater detail. Most people are infected with these negative beliefs about money so they're very susceptible to political platforms centered on taking from the rich to redistribute to the poor.

The two parties exploit this in their desire to remain or become the party in power. And the slippery slope begins. *We go from* Atlas Shrugged *the novel, to* Atlas Shrugged *the movie, to* Atlas Shrugged *the reality*.

Governments Have Become the New Ponzi Schemes

They're the ultimate pyramid money games. If you practiced the same accounting practices your government does, you would be put in prison.

Governments get away with this because they control the printing presses—and when money gets scarce, they simply print more. Which of course devalues all of the existing money even more, increases inflation, and drives up the cost of living. (And again, penalizes the poor worst of all.) But this allows the bureaucrats to continue kicking the can further down the road, with the only goal of winning the next election in order to maintain or regain power.

Know this: Unless a currency is backed by something (as the U.S. dollar was backed by gold until 1971), it is inherently worthless. It's just another mind virus. The government tells you a particular bill is worth 20 dollars or pounds or pesos, but that isn't true. That's just a subjective value they're trying to sell you, and the value declines every time they overspend and print more money. It's fiat currency; it works only when you buy into the bullshit. I'm just one of the lonely voices in the wilderness shouting, "The emperor has no clothes!"

Entitlement programs are now creating the opposite effect for which they were designed: Instead of helping the less fortunate work toward prosperity, they are enslaving those people in perpetual poverty. These well-meaning, but misguided programs have devolved into a vicious cycle, and politicians are exploiting the situation to pursue their agendas.

But You Can Prosper

So what are some things you can do to prosper in spite of these dangerous games being played by governments around the world?

Remember that every challenge presents a corresponding opportunity, often in disguise. But you can't assume that what worked in the past will work in the future. The pendulum may swing one way today, but it has to swing back at some point.

Play the status quo against itself.

When a commodity becomes scarce, value rises. When it becomes plentiful, value decreases. When a problem arises, people will pay dearly to resolve it. So, let's explore how you can make these circumstances work to manifest more success and prosperity in your life.

Disclaimer: I'm not an attorney or financial planner and I don't give legal or investment advice. Please find good legal and financial advisors who can assist you in your wealth-building goals.

I'm a prosperity coach. The only credential I can lay claim to is being a high-school dropout who got rich. I'll give you some concepts and ideas you can put into practice with your advisors, which brings us to my first rule of creating wealth:

If you want to become wealthy, don't seek financial advice from broke people.

A couple of years ago, I paid a lot of money to attend an investment conference in California. It was one of those "pitch-fests" that featured a different speaker every 90 minutes. They would try to sell you on their strategy for the first 30 minutes, and then spend the next 60 pitching their package for sale in the back of the room.

There was the real estate guy, the penny stock lady, the investment newsletter publisher, the Forex trader, and on and on. I sat through two days of this four-day program before I reached a startling conclusion: None of these experts presenting at this conference made more money than I did. So I called the airline, moved up my flight, and went home.

You have to manage your finances the same way. Your banker can probably give you some helpful advice on what kind of accounts you need. But she probably earns about $50,000 to $60,000 a year. So don't expect her to tell you how to become a millionaire.

Your accountant can probably offer you some solid strategies on reducing your tax liabilities. But if he's not financially free, don't expect him to teach you how to reach that goal. The same goes for your financial planner, stockbroker, and your cousins Pookie and Ray-Ray.

Retirement

Expecting your government to provide for your retirement is like getting menu-planning advice from Hannibal Lecter. Don't pay any attention to their figures and forecasts of what you will have. All pyramid schemes promise those kinds of returns.

And don't count on your company pension plan, either. Take a cue from all those airline employees who saw half of their retirement fund vaporized when their carrier filed for bankruptcy and got their pension fund obligations wiped away.

You have to take responsibility for your own prosperity and build enough of a retirement fund to live well. Anything you receive in a government or corporate pension is gravy you can use to gamble with or add to your Beanie Baby collection.

There are a few ways to do this:

Diversify

Do not put all of your retirement in one currency. You should be split into at least three or four different currencies. Remember these are all fiat currencies subject to political manipulation and public perception. In some countries, you can even set up your retirement fund to be in Swiss francs. (If the European Union really wanted to make the euro work, they should have modeled Switzerland. It's a country with four ethnicities and languages, financially strong cantons, and a single currency. Because they have reasonable privacy laws and aren't a war-mongering country, their currency is more stable than most.)

Don't keep all your assets where you live. You may think governments can't go bankrupt, but they can—and will. I like to think we can never have a run on the banks again, but that's a pretty optimistic outlook in light of current government fiscal policies.

If a banking system in a country collapses, the entire infrastructure goes right behind it. ATMs run out of cash, gas stations are sucked dry of fuel, and looters feel free to break into supermarkets and appliance stores. You have to be prepared for a currency to become worthless overnight or a country to become uninhabitable in a matter of weeks. Instead of a primary residence in Chicago and a vacation home in Florida, think of having your second residence in another country—preferably on another continent.

And Speaking of Real Estate . . .

Buy it. Great investment. Just make sure you do it the right way.

Forget all these crazy leverage deals with little or no money down. Put down a strong down payment or pay cash. If you finance, use a mortgage acceleration program and pay it off as soon as you can.

I know famed investor Robert Kiyosaki doesn't consider a home an asset, but I'd disagree with him. Owning property is good because land is another finite resource that will ultimately hold its value and appreciate.

Yes, real estate values will rise and fall, just like everything else. And while the subjective value of an area may fluctuate, values also run cycles. A property in a declining neighborhood might turn into a fortune when the area rebounds. And even given the market vagaries, land is still a limited resource whose value always seems to bounce back eventually.

The key is to never buy a property you will be forced to sell in a downturn. Put enough down so you could weather a one- or two-year downturn and still make the payments, even if you had no renters or renters who stay and don't pay. If you are able to wait out downturns like this, property will always rebound.

Be a Contrarian Thinker

Always be looking for which direction the masses are headed, and ask yourself what the pushback effect will be. (More about this in the next chapter.)

The more governments play games and devalue currencies, the more the value of precious metals like gold, silver, and platinum will rise. These metals are the only real currency in the world. Everything else is a promise to pay. And you can't trust the governments that are making the promises.

You should own some of all three precious metals I mentioned and continue to add them to your portfolio. And by own, I mean *take possession of the physical metals,* such as keeping gold bars in an easily accessed safe deposit box. Precious metals are the only real borderless currency.

Just like currencies, you don't want to keep all your precious metals in one country. I would keep most nearby, but have some in another country as well.

You can buy gold over the counter at an offshore bank or through a precious metals dealer. I like European banks because they are the most experienced at this, and renting a safe deposit box in Europe is quite inexpensive. These banks will usually want you to have an account there, but that's a good idea anyway. If you don't want to have an account with a foreign bank, you can store gold in a private vault.

There are two ways to buy gold in this medium: unallocated and allocated. *Unallocated*, also known as a *claim account*, is where the bank buys gold on your behalf. This is technically a "specific but undivided" situation. You would own a fractional interest in a 400-ounce gold bar. Stay away from this option because of the messiness of the ownership. (Also, when banks have become insolvent in the past, this gold has been considered an asset of the defunct bank and available to creditors.)

You are much better protected with *allocated* or, as it is sometimes called, *custodial storage*. The bank purchases your specific and divided gold off the books of the bank, meaning it is *your* asset, which they are simply storing for you. Purchase and storage costs are higher but worth the extra security.

I'm not recommending you buy and trade these bullion bars. That's for the day traders. You buy and hold them. Forever.

It doesn't matter what the market price is and how it goes up and down. You're looking for long-term security, not daily gains.

One other possibility to consider is precious metals certificates. My favorite of these is the Perth Mint Certificate. You buy the gold from wherever you are in the world, and they store it for you at the mint in Perth, Australia. (Like with the bank purchases, you can choose unallocated or allocated.) If you are a U.S. resident, you may want to check with a tax attorney but it appears that owning gold certificates does not require you to report that to the government as a foreign account.

The company that administers the program and stores your gold is owned by the State of Western Australia, who has guaranteed it will make good on any default by the company. It is one of the richest states in the country and, last time I checked, it had a AAA-rating from Standard and Poor's. So while I never really trust governments, I think that gives it a low-risk quality and allows you to diversify some assets overseas without flying to another country, physically taking gold to safe deposit boxes, and so on.

If you want to diversify even further, you might consider buying stocks of companies that mine precious metals. Their fortunes are tied to the price of the metals so the stocks respond accordingly.

Gold was almost $300 an ounce when I first started recommending that people buy it—and everyone thought I was crazy. I've never backed off, and even as it broke $500, $800, and $1,000 benchmarks, people kept deriding me. But I'm creating my future, not competing on *American Idol*.

Don't Listen to the Advice of Most People, Because Most People are Broke As a rule, commemorative gold and silver coins are not a good investment and don't justify the price they command. But you do want to have a small supply of them for an emergency. In case of a banking system meltdown, trading real gold or silver coins may be the only way to purchase fuel or food in a time of civil unrest. You can keep a small amount in your home safe and some extra in a nearby safe deposit box.

People still ask me if I think gold has peaked and will soon crash. All I know is I'm not selling any. With the current state of government budgets and currencies, I see no reason that gold can't go to $15,000 an ounce one day. I'm not saying it will, but I won't be surprised if it does.

Something Else to Keep in Mind . . .

When they start mining asteroids in space, gold may plummet to $200 an ounce! Someone will take the risk of investing in mining in outer space (Planetary Resources, whose investors include James Cameron and the Google boys, are already in the game), and could develop technology that allows them to bring precious metals back to earth cheaper than it costs to mine them here. That will change the markets in precious metals instantly.

And the same thing will happen in real estate. That oceanfront property you own in Florida will only continue to appreciate, because they're not making any more oceanfront land. But when developers start selling ocean-*floor* property, the market will adjust! And when developers start selling timeshares on the moon, the market will adjust again! And remember—we're not talking next century. For some of this, we're probably not even talking next decade. (Sir Richard Branson and his Virgin Galactic will be flying tourists into space starting in 2013.)

Taking Risks

What makes risky the new safe is taking calculated risks based on sound information and intelligent assumptions. It's doesn't mean that you take risks for the sake of risk. So as you prepare your portfolio, here's a simple guideline I use for allocating my own investments in terms of risk.

Put 50 percent of your portfolio in no-risk/low-reward investments. That means, theoretically, you can't lose your money; but of course, we know there are no absolutes in this case. The kind of investment I'm talking about is a savings account or certificate of deposit that comes with a government-backed guarantee. I do feel secure enough with precious metals to include them in this category.

A lot of sophisticated investors shun these low-reward investments because they're looking for higher yields. But that's why so many lost everything in the dot-com bubble, the real estate meltdown, or investing with Bernie Madoff.

I used to brag that if I lost everything, I would be a millionaire again within a year. Then I proved it. Then I decided it might be simpler if I just *didn't* lose everything.

The next step is to put 25 percent of your portfolio in moderate-risk/moderate-reward investments. This is where I'd classify things such as real estate and stocks.

And finally, you can put 25 percent of your portfolio into higher-risk/higher reward scenarios. This is when your cousin calls and tells you he's invested in an oil well and getting 2,000 percent return a year. Check it out and if it looks real, take the risk. But just because it works out for six months, don't take everything out of the other two categories and dump it into that. Pigs get fat. Hogs get slaughtered.

Bottom Line

Governments—even the well-meaning ones—are inherently corrupt and mismanaged. They never create prosperity— they squander or obstruct it. At best, they can facilitate an environment that allows free enterprise to prosper—and only free enterprise can create true prosperity.

The writing is on the wall: There will be serious economic upheaval caused by governments foolishly trying to micromanage economies. People who rely on governments for their retirement will get hurt. But for those who understand the reality of the situation, there are more opportunities than ever for creating wealth.

Tenor Aria

The New Religion
of Ideas

So far I've taken my speeches and workshops to more than 50 different countries, and that has presented a pretty fascinating dynamic.

I recently returned from Sofia, Bulgaria, where about 2,000 people paid quite a bit of money by their standards to come and hear my prosperity workshop. When I'm doing programs in Moscow, some people travel 30 hours by train or five days on the road—often sleeping in their cars—to attend. I did an all-day program in Kiev for 7,000 people in a gymnasium with no air conditioning where the temperature rose to over 100 degrees. Ten or 12 people left by ambulance with heat stroke, but nothing short of that was going to cause anyone else to leave.

Countries like Slovenia, Croatia, Macedonia, Latvia, and Lithuania are all facing a similar situation. Citizens of nations in countries where free enterprise was forbidden or held back by Socialist or Communist rule are now unleashing the pent-up demand for success they've had for decades. The level of passion, intensity, and urgency with which they attack opportunities is simply amazing to witness.

Books, and the authors who write them, are revered in these places, and seminars are considered life-changing experiences. People in some of these countries are so eager to get a photo or have a book signed that I need six bodyguards to get me out the backstage door and into the car safely.

The hunger they demonstrate is simply not apparent in most Western countries today. Offer a success seminar in London and you'll likely hear, "Too bad it's near Heathrow. Just can't fight that traffic. Let me know if you do one close to Gatwick." People in Miami think the 20 miles to Fort Lauderdale is too far to drive; people in Manhattan don't go to Queens, and Brooklynites won't take the ferry to Staten Island.

Now don't get me wrong: I'm blessed to have a lot of people who follow my work in the West, and they're very passionate about success and willing to do what's required for it. But if you take populations as a whole, comparing those in Western countries with those in former Soviet Bloc countries, you see a big ambition gap.

And it's widening . . .

The former Soviet Bloc countries (not to mention Asia) are embracing free enterprise with zeal, while the West is getting lazy. Too many people in the West take for granted the opportunities that free markets offer.

The other alarming trend in the West is the gradual but steady meltdown of the education system. Instead of teaching kids how to think—and yes, this is an actual skill that young people must learn—the system has deteriorated into teaching to the test. All this teaches students is that they have to memorize facts to get by.

Much of the curriculum taught in the West today is no longer relevant to the real world. Children don't need to be able to recite facts and dates. Any eight-year-old kid with a smartphone (and most do have them) can get that information within seconds. What young students need is an education that helps them develop critical thinking skills that will prepare them for the real world when they grow up.

What compounds the problem at the higher level is the fact that the university model is completely out of date. The physical model is built on books, classrooms, and sprawling campuses of brick and mortar, while the financial model is built on exploiting athletes, chasing endowments, and requiring students to go outrageously into debt to earn an accredited diploma.

By continuing to keep the focus on these things, universities are hastening their irrelevance.

A big reason for this is economics. Universities pursue endowments and hustle for cash, the biggest source of which is students who bet their future on huge student loans. The amount of debt of the average college graduate today is irrational. And more and more of these individuals will discover that the bet they made on their diploma getting them a good job was a bad wager.

Of course, universities will always have a place in our society. If you want to get a well-rounded education in languages, humanities, the arts, and philosophy, a university is probably still going to be the best place to find that. But *what* a university will be, and how such an institution will operate, will need to change dramatically.

It's no longer realistic to buy into the notion that you should borrow heavily against your future earnings to get a generalized degree, assuming the degree will lead to a job.

The accelerated speed of change has made it harder and harder for college curricula to remain relevant. And too many professors have experienced only what they teach in the vacuum of academia, not through actual experience in the real world. In the very near future, an MBA or PhD from a prestigious university is going to look fairly weak compared to a solid six-month, online training certificate in a specialized field like video game programming, mobile app design, or spaceship engine repair.

And how do you think savvy entrepreneurs like Mark Cuban, Richard Branson, or Mark Zuckerberg will weigh degrees and pedigrees versus real experience or relevance when they are hiring someone for their own companies? Well, here's a clue from *Blog Maverick*, Cuban's weblog:

> As an employer I want the best-prepared and qual-
> ified employees. I could care less if the source of
> their education was accredited by a bunch of old
> men and women who think they know what is best
> for the world. I want people who can do the job.
> I want the best and brightest. Not a piece of paper.

Education will evolve in the same way as the entrepreneurial world; those willing to think differently will find—and offer—great opportunity. North Carolina's High Point University tripled its enrollment because it daringly tackles some of these relevant issues: Preparing students for a future of both success and significance, going beyond training to a holistic education, curriculum with an emphasis on experiential learning, and a focus on valued-based living.

HPU has worked hard to be relevant in a rapidly changing world. This includes taking such actions as adding majors like interactive gaming; giving students more experience through internships; offering study possibilities in 25 countries; providing off-campus experiences in places like the stock exchanges to add context; and bringing in thought leaders like Malcolm Gladwell to address the student body.

It's no coincidence this renaissance at HPU is coming about under the direction of Dr. Nido Qubein, who took over as president in 2005. Nido comes from the real world of business. He arrived in the United States with $50 in 1966 and went on to reach extraordinary success as an entrepreneur. He helped start a bank in 1986, and today he chairs the executive committee of BB&T, a Fortune 500 financial corporation with $175 billion in assets and 35,000 employees. Nido is also chairman of Great Harvest Bread Company, a bakery with 218 stores across the country. He also serves on the boards of La-Z-Boy Corporation and fashion chain Dots Stores.

Nido acknowledged the challenges facing education during a conversation I had with him; however, he was excited to discuss how High Point is meeting these challenges. He said,

> The number of institutions will diminish and demand may indeed lessen. Transformative academies like HPU will prosper while transactional ones living only in the past may suffer. The real growth opportunity will be in making a college education affordable and available to the masses (who otherwise may not have pursued it). That is where you now see online classes and the like flourish.

The "Ivies" [Ivy League universities] will do fine in spite of everything, the HPUs (very few of them out there—we're close to unique in some ways) will grow because they are nimble, responsive, provide value, and interpret that value in ways that produce productive outcomes. The smaller schools that drown in an ocean of sameness may indeed meet very tough (if not catastrophic) times.

Yet, even forward-thinking institutions like High Point will need to reinvent a lot about what they do. You'll find a great deal of proud proclamations on their website about the huge increase in buildings and acreage on campus. How those kinds of investments will pay off in the digital world remains to be seen. (We can safely assume that at least one of those buildings is a library, housing books like dictionaries. The average kid today not only has no idea what a dictionary is, but would never have a need to know how to use one.)

We do know one thing for certain: Creating success in the new economy will require students to take much more responsibility for their own education. They'll need to make it less about degrees and more about practical application.

Nations such as India, Japan, Korea, and some other Asian countries are placing a renewed focus on education. They are churning out scores of college grads who are highly trained in very relevant fields like programming, gaming, biotechnology, environmental engineering, and entrepreneurship (taught by real entrepreneurs). Universities in the West will need to think more like High Point to regain relevance.

New World Order?

Take the passion for free enterprise you see demonstrated in the former Soviet Bloc countries, add in the focused attention to education in some of these countries, and you have the potential for a New World Order.

There are some small signs that the West is waking up—and hopefully this trend will continue. But right now, the advantage goes to a lot of the smaller, developing countries. Outsourcing will continue to expand, but instead of using this approach to take advantage of a cheaper work force, companies will be outsourcing to tap into a better-educated and more motivated labor pool.

So Where Does All This Take Us Right Now?

Disruptive technology is eliminating millions of jobs and requiring drastic changes to others. Cloning, along with other advances in medical technology and longevity, will shake things up even more. The irresponsible government financial policies we discussed in the last section are threatening the world economy.

Power is shifting from the West to developing and even third-world countries. The education system is not preparing you or your kids for how to succeed in the new economy. So just how can people and companies compete and remain relevant in the new world order?

The New Religion of Ideas

All true prosperity springs from the power of ideas. (If you are interested in the metaphysical process behind this, read *Prosperity* by Charles Fillmore.) Because the education system has lost the plot, people's critical thinking ability is shrinking and ideas are diminishing.

The most valuable, cherished, and sought-after currency in the new economy will be **ideas**.

Savvy employees will create their own critical thinking curriculum that incorporates a mélange of problem solving, lateral thinking, logic, and creativity. People who do this will become idea generators and declare themselves free agents. Just like superstar athletes, they'll be able to entertain a variety of offers and choose the most lucrative long-term deal.

The future still lies in education—just not in the way we know it now.

Because I never finished high school, I'll admit my experience with formal education is quite limited. When I was 30 years old, I took some college courses for about a year and a half to keep myself challenged. I was amazed at how little college actually prepares you for the real world—and I was incredulous that it seems to follow the same model of high school and primary school: *It programs you with* **what** *to think, instead of teaching you* **how** *to think*.

Higher education still leads you to believe that learning is about memorizing facts, which I think is actually the least important element in education. The most essential areas relevant to education in the new economy will be:

- Curiosity
- Discipline
- Discernment
- Contrarianism

Let's look at each of these in greater detail.

Curiosity   It shouldn't come as a surprise that curiosity is important to a good education. This is what creates the passion for learning. The most intellectually developed people are also the most curious. A guy named Einstein once said, "I have no special talent. I am only passionately curious." And he seemed to be a pretty bright fellow.

If you want to grow and develop, you must maintain your childlike curiosity about the world around you, because curiosity drives us to knowledge. However, being curious is just the beginning. You also need the second trait we mentioned . . .

Discipline   Casual curiosity ignites the spark of learning and leads you to investigate ideas and topics that have surface interest for you. But any learning of real substance requires discipline. It will require you to go deeper and study subjects that don't seem as intriguing at first, but truly make you think.

I have a CD series on the great philosophies of the world. I have another one of the principles of the Objectivist philosophy. They both give me a headache, literally. When I listen to them, I have to pause and replay, stop and look up words in the dictionary, or just take a breather to process what I just heard so that often I actually *do* get a headache.

But that's the good kind of headache, the one that comes from stretching your brain around new concepts, learning new vocabulary, and developing new thought processes. These things are the sure signs of growth and enlightenment.

But just being exposed to enlightening material is not enough. You must employ the third trait from the list ...

Discernment What a lost art this is today. So many people have worthiness and self-esteem issues that they desperately look for others to tell them what to think. This takes away the pressure of having to make decisions, discern truth from fiction, and actually think for themselves.

But you have to do better ...

When you are exposed to new information, you must process it first through your powers of discernment. This is the ability to form opinions by objectively evaluating the information presented to you. This facility is what allows you to make good judgments. But that doesn't happen if you blindly accept *all* the information presented to you. Intelligent people realize everything presented to them (including this book) comes shaded with some bias. And that leads us to the last very critical trait of enlightened learning ...

Being a Contrarian Because sometimes even discernment isn't enough. Sometimes you have to see the world in a totally different way than the rest of the herd.

The reality is most people today are automatons, blindly following the herd through the motions of life. They are merely existing—not living. Most people today are not happy, healthy, or successful. So why would you want to think like them? You don't. Or you'll end up like them. So don't be afraid to be contrary to what everyone seems to be doing. In fact, be afraid if you're not. Not only is risky the new safe in the new economy; weird is the new normal.

This means individuals will take a personal responsibility for their own education. It will likely include elements of the traditional education system but will also require an additional mix of alternative, experiential, and contrarian content.

Playing to Win in the Shark Tank

For companies, the most important resource in which to invest will become people. Of course, many companies claim that they already do this—but that is simply window dressing. This investment will need to become deeply integrated in the corporate culture.

For HR departments, the focus will shift to stronger recruiting, more vetting, and creating the best free-agent packages. Of course, a lot more of these workers will be independent contractors. But all of them will need to be wooed and paid based upon what they bring to the table. Your success as a human resources manager will be judged on your ability to sign the premier free agents.

I believe you'll see a return to companies encouraging employees to continue their education and even be willing to participate in the cost. But just as athletes have to refund a portion of their signing bonus if they walk away, don't be surprised to see companies requiring a certain amount of service in return for what they invest in an employee's or contractor's education.

Keynote speakers, trainers, and consultants will see increased demand, but they'll provide more and more of their services from the cloud.

Results-Based Compensation

The changes we're discussing will increase accountability for both employees and employers, and that's a good thing. The days of keeping your head low and hiding out in a cubicle are over. You'll see more and greater focus placed on results-based compensation. Employees will be required to demonstrate value; and to keep the good performers, companies will need to show they aren't just running a slash-and-burn operation to generate higher dividends every quarter.

The new order companies won't be in industries like manufacturing, medicine, or even technology. The most powerful companies will be in education and information—more specifically, helping people and companies process the overwhelming avalanche of information to which they are exposed.

These new order companies and the people who work in them will need to become more innovative, change faster, and be willing to take risks. They'll also have to be much smarter, because the speed at which change is happening is now so fast, being nimble won't be enough. As we discussed in Act I, reacting fast will not be sufficient. You have to foresee trends and be one of the first people to adopt them.

Creativity will be king, and ideas will drive that creativity. Those ideas are what will allow you to enjoy success in a rapidly changing world. In the next act we'll explore a strategy they aren't teaching yet in the business schools: how to move fast and break things!

Act III

Move Fast and Break Things

That quote I used for the chapter title was the daily mantra for Mark Zuckerberg and the Facebook clan as they grew their company from a modest networking website for college kids into the largest social media juggernaut in the world.

Breaking things may be risky, but in the new space, playing safe pretty much guarantees you will fail.

Down is up, and up is down. All of the developments we've discussed thus far have redefined not only what success is, but how you get there today. People hanging on to the past will get left behind, but people who are willing to move fast and break things will succeed at levels we have yet to see.

Here's a small, but mind-bending cross section of how some of these challenges actually offer great opportunities.

The New Reality of Marketing

We now live in the age of overload. The human brain has never had to process as much information as it is required to today. The average person is besieged with a torrent of distracting stimuli 24/7. As a result, their attention span is shorter and their defenses stronger. Entrepreneurs need to rethink the ways in which they reach their audiences—and so far, they're doing a horrible job.

Conventional wisdom says that direct mail is dead. Yet when I promote my prosperity seminars, I get a very good response from mail campaigns. Why? Because since all the other seminar providers believe the medium is dead, they aren't using it. They're happily patting themselves on the back, thinking how much money they're saving by eliminating printing and postage from their budget.

It's yet another example of how when everyone is zigging, you want to be zagging.

But you still have to be smart. Take the other side of the equation: I bought my condo in Miami Beach from a doctor. That was over six years ago, and every week I get at least one and sometimes several pieces of bulk mail addressed to him promoting some medical conference, equipment, or drug.

You would think periodically running your mailing list through the change-of-address check with the postal service would be a basic rule of Marketing 101. (On average, 2 percent of the people on any list will die or move each month.) But there are at least 50 marketers in the medical field who haven't done this *even once* in six years. Statistically, every single person on their list has moved or died by now—and one in five has moved or died twice!

These marketers are probably lamenting their declining response rates and take them as proof that direct mail no longer works. Direct mail still works great—just not in the same way it did 20 years ago.

These company executives are probably having meetings with advertising agencies who tell them they can save all that money by building an email database. But there's a problem with that: Email is actually another medium that is facing declining results—one that will either die or have to be radically reengineered.

A growing number of people are moving from email to texting, a trend that's likely to continue. Not to mention the exponential growth of social media and microblogging. My nieces and nephews haven't sent me an email in years, but I hear from them all the time via Facebook messages. Five- and six-year-olds now use iPads to call each other, using apps like FaceTime. They would think email was old fashioned—if they had ever heard of it.

The old-school interruption marketers are doing crazier and bolder things to try and break through the clutter. Much of this is just plain silly, and gets attention, but in the wrong way, and from the wrong people.

These same people have jumped into social media because they see it as simply another platform to broadcast their message at people. They don't understand the nuances of the various sites and completely miss out on the listening and engagement aspects those sites offer. (For help on understanding this better, check out the book *UnMarketing* by Scott Stratten.)

Unfortunately, you can't swing a dead cat today without hitting at least five people who claim to be "social media experts." They believe that following 2,000 random people a day on Twitter to see who follows back or knowing how to set up a Facebook fan page makes them a guru in this field. Yet most of them offer dreadful advice that perpetuates the most common mistakes people are making. And while giving someone a coupon or premium to "like" your Facebook page isn't a bad thing, you need to establish some plan for what you're going to do after that.

Social media changes everything in the equation. However, it's not just another channel you can use to shout your message at people.

Social media has dramatically changed the way customers find you, vet you, and buy from you, as well as the way *you* find, vet, and buy. It eliminates the need for many middlemen (and therefore, the need for many jobs); it makes controlling a brand or image dramatically more problematic; and it can drive prices down. On the flip side, social media has a lot of wonderful things going for it. It lets you connect directly with your tribe, monitor your brand in real time, and immediately alerts you to any problems in the marketplace. But where it *really* changes the game is in branding.

The Real Truth on Branding

Card-carrying contrarian Joe Calloway has a brilliant take on branding. Instead of trying to lead in your category, he advocates creating a new category and being the only one in it. His book, *Becoming a Category of One*, is a thought-provoking look at competitive positioning well worth your time.

Navigating the minefield of branding and positioning has never been an easy path. Now things are getting more complex. You never could really control your brand in the past, but you could at least try. Social media has made that virtually impossible. The difference now is you really know what your brand actually represents in the marketplace and when you need to fix something. (Required reading on the subject: *Building Brand Value* by Bruce Turkel.)

Your brand is not your logo or corporate colors, and it really isn't even about your product or service. Your brand is a *reflection of* your product or service. It's how the market perceives you. And that is created by the customer's *experience* with your product or service. The Internet allows people to share those experiences more readily, and that has impacted brands in a big way.

And social media has made branding really interesting.

On the surface, your brand is how the market perceives you. On a deeper level, it's how the market perceives *what you can do for them*. But at the ultimate, ultimate level— and now we're in the rarified air of brands like Apple, Cirque du Soleil, Starbucks, and Nike—your brand is *how you make the consumer feel about him- or herself.*

That 350-pound guy you see taking the escalator? He would get winded in a chess match. But in his mind, he's an elite athlete, because he's wearing a sweatshirt that says, "Just Do It!"

I'm a bald, middle-aged, white guy, but I use a Mac. So when I walk in that Apple store, with all those skater kids, people with their dogs, and the rad guys in the Genius Bar, I feel cool!

The same is true for the people you see in line for their half-decaf, double-mocha-froth, carmelata-Frappuccinos at Starbucks; the ones browsing around in the Apple superstores; and those mesmerized by a performance of

Cirque du Soleil. They are passionate advocates of the product they are buying—or more accurately, *experiencing*. They believe in what they buy and want to share their experience with everyone they know. They move from customers to a marketing team more powerful than any amount of money can ever buy. This is the epitome of what Seth Godin describes in his brilliant book *Tribes*.

When your brand inspires a tribe, it can make you rich. And nothing inspires a tribe more than making people feel a certain way about themselves. Nike makes everyone feel like an elite jock; Starbucks admits you into the clubhouse; Apple lets you be one of the cool kids; and Cirque takes you to an enchanted place.

Chrysler did this brilliantly with their Viper brand. (In fact, they did it so successfully that they were seriously trying to sell it as a stand-alone company when they faced bankruptcy.) They created and currently manage a worldwide Viper Club with local chapters, host a website and e-zine, post videos, and print a glossy magazine. The "Members Only" section of the site includes blogs and boards where the tribe connects and builds deeper fervor in the brand. Every year or two, Chrysler hosts "Viper Owners Invitationals," which are basically conventions for us American muscle-loving, testosterone-crazed, speed demons.

Stop by one of these events and watch all the key chains, jackets, replica models, and other gee-gaws the attendees buy. Go into the Cirque store after a performance and see how fast people are snapping up $125 t-shirts. As a member of both these tribes, I can attest to the after effect.

I have my Viper caps, racing jackets, polo shirts, custom floor mats, gearshift knobs, miniature models, posters, clocks, and books. I can even drink my Dr. Pepper (another tribe I belong to) from my Viper coffee mugs or engraved Viper glasses, set on my engraved Viper logo coasters. (No, I am not kidding.) Additionally, I could stock a small boutique with all the Cirque clothes I've got, and I have the program, CD, and DVD for every show I've ever seen.

We all buy these things because we want to take a little piece of the show home with us and relive how it made us feel. True branding was always about this. Now technology and social media simply make it easier (or harder, if you don't get it) and make it all happen faster.

And since we're talking tribes, branding, and using tech to facilitate the process—and since I'm writing this book down in Key West, Florida—I would be remiss if we didn't do a case study on one of the most brilliant proponents of all this: singer Jimmy Buffett.

I'm a card-carrying member of the Parrot Head tribe (which for you heathens who don't know, are Jimmy Buffett fans). So for dinner last night, I walked over to Duval Street and had a "Cheeseburger in Paradise" at Jimmy's Margaritaville Cafe.

Buffett has done such a magnificent job leading his tribe and harnessing the power of technology, he should command a course in every business school. He isn't trying to save the world; however, he has managed to lead a movement that can make it a happier place for us all. His tribe is about fun, music, and giving back.

Before anyone else made CD-ROMs, Jimmy put them on the flip side of his CDs for computer-literate Parrot Heads.

Although he's had a lot of chart hits, you almost never hear a new Buffett song on the radio. Because his music defies categorization—it's country, it's reggae, it's jazz, it's pop—station music directors aren't sure what to do with it. Like a lot of people in the corporate world, they simply do what everyone else does, so they play the same old hits and don't take a chance on the new stuff, despite the millions of fans who would love to hear Jimmy's voice coming through the radio.

So Jimmy skipped the traditional radio and record company distribution channel and took his movement directly to the people. He set up his own studio and his own label. Year after year he tours the globe, along with his Coral Reefer Band, selling out venue after venue, without any of the normal promotion. He writes books that have become best sellers and releases album after album, DVD after DVD, which fans keep snapping up.

Jimmy also embraced the Internet way before the rest of the music industry. He created his Internet radio station, Radio Margaritaville, in 1998. In 2005, it became the first Internet station to transition to mainstream radio when it became a channel on Sirius Satellite Radio. (It's also available on iTunes.) The station plays a casual mix of beach music, reggae, and, of course, a steady diet of Jimmy's hits.

Long before the rest of the music business got it, Jimmy was streaming all of his concerts over Radio Margaritaville for free. (Yet, a Parrot Head would *never* think to knock off a Buffett album.) And instead of hurting concert attendance, these free Internet offerings drive even *more* traffic to the live shows. Each event is packed with the tribal faithful, sporting Parrot Head hats, fins, grass skirts, and other trinkets connected with their favorite Buffett songs.

Before each concert Jimmy does a live tailgate party on Radio Margaritaville, talking about the venue, set list, any guest stars, and just generally being a raconteur. It may be the best demonstration of how to use social media and technology to engage with a tribe that you'll ever see.

Jimmy gets it. It's not about selling records or tickets to concerts; it's about creating an experience. But here's the key: that experience really isn't about *him*. It's about how he makes his fans feel (rebellious, a little naughty, and young again). And that is the ultimate branding.

Of course, just when you think you've got the music business figured out, Mark Cuban is trying to change it again. AXS TV (Cuban's venture with Ryan Seacrest Media, CAA, and concert promoter AEG) is in the market with a business model combining love concerts, pay-per-view broadcasts, and DVD/Blu-ray releases. They partner with artists to do live events, which AXS TV broadcasts as they happen, and give the footage to the artist for physical products. I recently received a similar proposal from a media company for my seminars. You'll see a lot more partnerships like this in music, other entertainment, and education.

Spreading Memes through the Internet

A brand is really a meme-plex—a collection of related memes, aka mind viruses. And nothing spreads memes faster than the Internet. When Nike creates a YouTube sensation like "Write the Future" or when, in the near past, millions of people tuned in to see Steve Jobs launch a new product—whenever someone tweets, posts a review on a website, updates their Facebook status, or adds a pin about their new iPad, memes are flying and branding is taking place.

Older, established companies lament the fact they can't control their brand. Smart entrepreneurs will realize that is a good thing. Because while you can't control your brand, you can actually monitor it in real time, exactly as it's playing out in the market. You can become aware of problems the moment they occur, help the people having difficulties, make corrections, and turn potentially lost customers into raving advocates.

Let's look at a few examples of how this happens in the real world.

One year I bought some last-minute Christmas presents from retailer Hammacher Schlemmer because they guaranteed delivery by December 24. Imagine my chagrin when I called my nieces and nephews on Christmas day only to discover they hadn't received anything. So naturally, I wrote a newsletter article titled "Hammacher Schlemmer—The Grinch Who Stole Christmas."

A few days later, I received a call from the president of Hammacher Schlemmer. First, he apologized profusely for the mix up, and while he didn't make excuses, he explained to me how the mistake happened. He also asked my permission to reprint my newsletter, issue it to every customer service representative in the company, and make it required reading for new hires. Oh, and a week later, the kids got all of their presents—at no charge to me. I went from someone who would have never ordered from them again to someone who has since spent thousands of dollars with them.

When I was doing a speech in Valencia, Spain, I tweeted about how beautiful the city and architecture were. Five minutes later I got a message from the Valencia Visitor and Convention Bureau welcoming me to the city and providing a link to a website showing all the local attractions. You might wonder how they tracked me, but it's really pretty simple stuff. You just get an application like TweetDeck and keep a search column for certain keywords. Yet almost no one does it!

One day I was venting in my blog about the fact that the Ritz Carlton in Singapore hadn't given me the regular suite I had requested, and the room they had given me had no hangers for a suit. Thirty minutes after I posted this, I received a frantic email from a VP at Ritz to make things right. Turns out his mother reads my blog, and she wasn't very happy!

Examples like these demonstrate how organic brands really are, and how the web and social media can influence them in a matter of moments. They show how you can turn a bad situation into a great one.

Then there's the other side of the story . . .

I can't count the number of times I've tweeted about surly service, dirty planes, or late arrivals on American Airlines. Obviously American can't either, since they've never responded to any of them.

Of course, I do get scores of replies from other frustrated elite flyers in their frequent flier program and lots of messages from loyal Southwest customers urging me to switch. (And I love you, Herb Kelleher, but that ain't happening until you guys add a first class!) If you want more dialogue, you need only go to the message boards at Insideflyer.com or search any of the other social media sites to learn what hundreds of other aggravated American customers have to say. Someone from the C suite at American could do the same thing—*if* they cared. *Note:* Now that they've filed for bankruptcy, they have just recently started responding to tweets. Of course, it's a little late.

I'm certainly not the only social media–savvy traveler, who takes out his frustrations in cyberspace. The image on the next page is an example from blogger Aaron Strout, with a little happier ending.

If I were running an airline today, I would employ one high-level customer service agent whose only responsibility would be to manage the company's Twitter account, blog, and Facebook page (jointly branded with the airline's name, a picture, and title, along with the company logo) and *then subscribe to the feeds of every single elite-level member of their frequent flyer program*. That's all public information; it would only take some searching.

And speaking of untapped opportunities, have you seen what a tragic disaster the day-to-day operation of the airline industry has become? Airplane seats were designed when people were about five feet tall. Now a lot of teenagers are pushing over six feet, and more than half the population is overweight, many by a lot. Yet the airlines are shoehorning even more seats into cramped, dingy cabins. They're charging you to call the reservation line, check your suitcase, select a seat, and they'd dock you for using the bathroom if they thought they could get away with it.

CommonSense
FOR TODAY'S COMPANY

HOME   ABOUT   AUTHORS   PUBLISHED CONTENT   KEY INSIGHTS   ARCHIVES   EVENTS   COMMON

What Does It Cost to Say I'm Sorry?

Posted by: Aaron Strout **in** Communication Strategy, Customer Experience, Integrated Communications, Pre-Commerce, Public Relations Practice, Social Media Insights & Trends, Thinking Creatively **on June 13, 2012**

As a rule of thumb, I try not to ever use social media to bash a brand. It's just not productive and who knows, one day I may end up pitching that company for business. Once in a while I may publicly express frustration with a brand — not in the hopes that I'll get something from them — but to either warn friends or to let a company know that they have messed up. Unfortunately, last night one of those opportunities cropped up at the tail end of my flight from Austin to San Francisco.

101
tweets

TOP ★ 5K
retweet

> **Aaron Strout** @AaronStrout   15h
> Hey @USAirways, thanks a bunch for making me wait 40 minutes for my CARRY ON bag. That's why I don't check luggage. #gatecheckfail
> Details

> **US Airways** @USAirways   [Follow] [person]
>
> @AaronStrout Sorry about that Aaron. We know your time is valuable and will forward your feedback to our baggage team. ^SV
>
> ← Reply   ⇄ Retweet   ★ Favorite
> 7:38 AM - 13 Jun 12 via SocialEngage · Embed this Tweet

> Reply to @USAirways @AaronStrout

> **Aaron Strout** @AaronStrout   4h
> .@USAirways thank you. Your apology means a lot to me.
> Details

By way of background, I find myself flying more and more with U.S. Airways. In the past, I've been somewhat ambivalent toward them. They were good, not great. They didn't have wifi or television. No blue potato chips and their flights from Austin to Phoenix (the stopover on the

Imagine what an opportunity there is for an airline that brings the comfort and glamour back to air travel. (Although to be fair, yesterday I flew Aeroflot, of all carriers, and passengers were greeted by three flight attendants offering newspapers and magazines—wearing hats, white gloves, and high heels! It took me back to the halcyon days of Pan Am.)

Everyone focuses on customer acquisition when the real money is in customer retention—and social media can help companies retain customers in numerous and wondrous ways. You can connect with your tribe, build a deeper relationship, and create a bonding experience like never before. (And of course, the savviest entrepreneurs will extend this into the mobile app field.) It allows the personalization and emotional connection that simply wasn't possible before.

Just as Jimmy Buffett built his brand with his fans, young electronic music producers like Skrillex and Deadmau5 (pronounced "dead mouse," but if you're cool, you already know that) are harnessing technology to do the same thing. They post free audio and video downloads, participate in social media, and stream webcasts to connect with an ever-growing legion of fans. These guys are selling out stadiums with frenzied fans for their techno shows. They offer early releases to their loyal followers and utilize the technology of social media brilliantly. Already by 2009, Deadmau5's performances were recorded and made available for sale immediately following his concerts on wristband USB flash drives.

All of this tech offers the opportunity for small and nimble entrepreneurs to outplay huge competitors. Right now, most large companies don't have a clue about social media or mobile. ("Janet, get us one of the QR code things.")

They see them both as necessary evils they have to do because everyone else is doing them. Or worse, they think of them as two more channels they can use to broadcast press releases. Their PR departments set up a Twitter account for the president or CEO and then some clueless employee tweets in their name. Or they establish a corporate account and simply broadcast press releases and sales pitches. No one is monitoring the feed, listening, or interacting.

The perfect case study of a little guy taking on the big boys and cleaning their clocks is what video blogger and speaker Gary Vaynerchuk did with Wine Library TV. He used a daily video blog to grow a mom-and-pop liquor store into an online retailer grossing $45 million annually. Here are just a few of the many things he does right:

- Is transparent and real.
- Offers real value instead of pitching.
- Listens and responds to his market.
- Works his face off.

Any employee or entrepreneur can learn great lessons from what Gary did—and how he did it. Be sure to read his book, *Crush It!*

The other thing social media does is allow you to create market demand from the bottom up. Gary did this in the retail world with wine, and I did it in the corporate market for my business as a professional speaker and consultant.

About five years ago, I decided to really take a hard look at social media and do some critical thinking on how it would play out in terms of building a business. I came to the conclusion that it would be the single most productive strategy I could utilize.

The first step was becoming active via my blog at RandyGage.com. It seemed to me that the most popular bloggers posted daily, so I started putting up five posts a week. This allowed me to form a great connection with my tribe and helped to grow my reach in a big way. Today my blog is in the top 1 percent of the world in terms of traffic.

Yet you'll notice that I never use it to pitch, because I know this isn't what my readers want. (Although by the time you're reading this, all bets are off, since I'll be relentlessly hawking this book!) Seriously, I consistently provide tons of free value. Then, when I come out with a new book or seminar or other resource, I'll announce it, but in a way that still offers value. The blog brings lots of visitors to my site. If they like my work, they look around the rest of the site and usually end up buying something.

Next, I began participating in social media sites. I started by launching a Twitter account and learned how that site worked while my number of followers continued to rise. After about a year, I got serious about Facebook and started putting up a couple posts a day and interacting with people.

It became apparent to me that video was going to be the real driver, so the next step was to get more active on You-Tube. I started putting up a show occasionally and got a little traction. As I studied the serious players, most of them were doing a show a week. I modeled that and then things really began taking off there. These days I'm exploring Pinterest and Google+. I'm a little too edgy for the corporate world, so I don't do a lot with LinkedIn, but the corporate people I know swear by it. The other very intriguing possibility right now is Airtime, which is basically Twitter with video. It has the possibility to be the next big thing, simply because it's video-based instead of text-based.

I got to the point where I spent two hours every day on social media. Most people in my profession say they don't have that kind of time. But it's the best investment I've ever made. Not only have I formed strong connections with thousands of people around the world who follow my work, but I have scores of loyal fans who actually *drive business* for me. I have found my tribe, and they have found me. (This book is the result of them imploring me to write it.)

I haven't had a marketing packet for my speaking business for three years. I've never solicited a consulting job in my life. And I never make cold calls or seek business. My tribe *creates* business for me. They practically demand their meeting planner book me as a speaker at their conferences or insist that the CEO bring me in to work with the company. And this is the beauty of authentically engaging in social media: Instead of chasing after business, getting active on these platforms will get business chasing after *you*.

This all means that controlling your brand and reputation is harder if you're not actively monitoring and participating in social media—but it's actually easier if you are. And ultimately this new environment is better for everyone. Now, the only way to really control your brand is the right way: by providing great products or services, engaging with customers, and resolving complaints in a timely manner.

The Real Sweet Spot

There's one place where the winners will separate from the losers: *scalability*. If you're a financial planner, speaker, or hair stylist, running your social media and online relationships is a simple enough equation. It's not *easy*, but it is simple. But if you're a hotel chain, automaker, or movie studio, it's neither easy nor simple. That's because bigger companies like these require the executive level to really get behind social media, both online and mobile. Not with lip service and mission statements, but by actually instilling it deeply into the culture of the business and getting every employee involved.

It will mean sorting out the nebulous lines between personal posting versus company positions, branding accounts with people versus company departments and other issues. This will take some discernment, and it will be different for every company and entrepreneur. (Note that if you're an attorney or financial planner—or a law, accounting, or financial planning firm—there are serious legal issues that you need to consider regarding social media posts.)

Nobody wants to follow a Twitter account or Facebook page from the ExxonMobil marketing department, but they may like one from Mary in marketing. It's probably good and adds personality if Mary expresses her undying love for the Red Sox, but not so good if she updates her views on gay adoption.

There are no fixed rules for this now. We'll all be sorting them out for the next few years. Many old companies will disappear, because this new approach to branding and marketing will expose their mediocrity. They'll be replaced by authentic companies that embrace social media and have nothing to fear from transparency. This will give a much greater degree of power to the consumer and actually result in better companies and business practices.

Retail Is Dead

Okay, it's not dead yet, but retail is becoming less relevant every week. And that's not surprising, since the business model for retail hasn't really changed at all in at least a couple hundred years.

Goods used to be manufactured in England and transported by ship to the New World. They arrived at ports like Boston and New York, and then traveled by stagecoach across the country for delivery to general stores, where the consumer came in and purchased them. Ships turned into planes, stagecoaches turned into trains and 18-wheelers, and general stores turned into department stores and shopping malls, but the business model stayed the same. In fact, we could really argue it got more cumbersome, as layers of rack jobbers, wholesalers, and warehousing got involved in the process.

The endless parade of retailers filing for bankruptcy shouldn't surprise anyone. What other industry is still trying to use the same business model in 2012 as they were using in 1776?

There are two business models that pose the greatest threat to retail: One surprising and misunderstood by most, the other predictable and also misunderstood by most. The first is multi-level or network marketing, and the second is online retailing. Let's look at what the future likely holds in store for each of them.

Network Marketing

Network marketing (often called MLM, short for multi-level marketing) as we know it today began, for all practical purposes, in 1956 when Dr. Forest Shaklee started the Shaklee Corporation, and two childhood friends, Jay Van Andel and Richard DeVos, founded what later morphed into the Amway Corporation. Since then, network marketing and its sister profession, direct selling, have grown steadily in acceptance and sales. The business has survived the pyramid schemes, chain letters, and money games of the seventies and eighties and emerged as a serious player. Right now MLM companies are moving fast and breaking things to the tune of $28 billion annually in the United States and $117 billion worldwide.

The skepticism that surrounded the business for so long has been replaced with acceptance. Millions of people have become involved, mainstream media has started to notice, and there are lots of proven results to offer. American business magnate Warren Buffett's Berkshire Hathaway now owns three companies in the business, and he has been quoted as saying that, dollar for dollar, it's the best investment he's ever made. That's quite a statement for someone widely considered to be the most successful investor of the twentieth century. (And for those of you keeping score at home, I just referenced both Buffetts in the same chapter!) Although popular folklore says the Oracle of Omaha and the Minstrel of Margaritaville are related (and they call each other Cousin Jimmy and Uncle Warren)—they're actually not. Although as *Fortune* magazine noted in a 1999 piece, both play stringed instruments, stick to their guns, and are filthy rich!

Besides me, other financial and success authors like Robert Kiyosaki and David Bach have been recommending the business for years.

The Golden Era of Network Marketing   Now, we are about to enter the golden era of network marketing.

In the next few years alone, tens of millions of new distributors will join the network marketing profession. And as much as companies like to suggest they are heading for an exponential growth curve, when sales increases are almost vertical, it's likely *the profession as a whole* will experience that growth cycle. There are lots of indicators and trends suggesting this will be the case.

First, we need look no further than the current broken model of retail distribution today, with all its needless parasites between the manufacturer and the consumer. Contrast that with the elegant model of network marketing, where the company that manufactures a product ships it directly to a distributor. This person is often either the end consumer or someone who conversationally markets it to family, neighbors, and friends. (And if you don't know how this works, you haven't been on Facebook lately!)

The money that retailers of the regular retail model normally waste on advertising and unnecessary layers of distribution is instead spent on product research and development (R&D) and sharing the profits with those who actually do the work and provide value.

Network marketing is the ultimate results-based compensation, because it's a business where people are paid exactly what they're worth.

The other big advantage of network marketing is the social aspect. MLM is like social media on steroids, in 3-D and living color! Every product is presented along with a personal testimonial from someone you know and trust. It's done in small home meetings, one-on-one encounters in coffee shops, and through friend networks on social media sites.

It's for this reason that many health and nutritional products found their way into mainstream consciousness through network marketing. If they just sat on a grocery or health food store shelf, no one would buy them because people needed to be educated about products before making a purchase. Network marketing is perfect for this, and it's the perfect distribution model for the new economy.

Think about the millions of jobs we know will be eliminated by advances in technology, and the millions more that will require the people who have them to radically retrain themselves in order to keep them. For example, a detective used to get trained by working a beat as a patrol officer, but soon they're going to have to be experts in biotechnology and DNA. In another case, the promotion for a simple pack-and-pick warehouse job may go to the people who can lift and stack 400-pound boxes quicker, which they do because they're more proficient with the powered exoskeleton suit they're wearing. A large number of these people are likely to seek out business opportunities—and the benefits that network marketing provides will appeal to many.

Now think of the millions more layoffs that will occur because of governments having to face reality and make hard choices to move toward balanced budgets. Some countries will actually go bankrupt; others will slash pensions and entitlements to the bone. Millions of people will recognize that they cannot trust their futures or retirement to government, and many of them will also see network marketing as a vehicle to proactively protect their future.

It's conceivable that 40 or 50 million new people will become network marketing distributors in the period from 2013 to 2017, as all this economic upheaval is taking place. It took almost 60 years for network marketing to reach $100 billion in sales. The second $100 billion will likely be reached in only 10 or 15 years. And that $200 billion could easily double to $400 billion in five to seven years after that. For the most part these are not new sales—they are coming out of existing channels, mainly retail.

The Next Dot-Com Bubble

The next dot-com bubble won't really be a bubble, but the logical migration of a huge swath of purchasing from the retail environment to the online world. We can (hopefully) assume that this time around, companies and investors will not lose sight of the necessity of delivering a quality product at a fair price that also allows for a profit.

The thing most often overlooked about e-commerce today is the beginning. Not the yeas-ago beginning, but the *real* beginning, meaning the one that's starting right now.

The statistics you read about online commerce may seem mind-boggling, and they grow substantially every season, but you have to keep in mind that we are still at the very, *very* earliest of stages of online purchasing right now. Those huge sales figures you see reported today are miniscule in comparison to what they will be 5 and 10 years from now.

This massive migration to online buying will cause two very different demands on entrepreneurs.

First, of course, will be the necessity of brick and mortar retailers to remain relevant and create a reason for people to still come to them. Stores and malls won't go away, but they will have to do a lot of things differently. It's possible no one has done this better thus far than Tesco (or demonstrated a better use of QR codes). In Korea they faced the challenge of competing with other supermarket chains with more stores in better locations. Their solution: virtual stores in places like subway stations.

They have set up displays that looked just like their actual stores, except they are simply large photos on banners. Shoppers use their smartphones to scan the QR code on the picture of the item they want, select a quantity, and add it to their virtual cart. Once they finish shopping, they complete the order, and it's delivered shortly after

they get home. (You can see a great case study here: http://
simplesells.tumblr.com/post/24044870654/ homeplus).

The other demand will be on the existing and
emerging online retailers. They have to create an online
experience (or more likely, a mobile one) that's compa-
rable to retail and better than other online retailers.

Put another way, physical retailers will need to
mimic the convenience of online buying, and online
retailers will need to mimic the social aspects of the stores
and malls. And of course, the savvy ones will be operating
seamlessly through *both* channels. Some companies, like
Apple and clothing retailer Andrew Christian, are already
doing this well. The majority of both brands' sales take
place online, with the rest done in iconic flagship stores.

Amazon is absolutely crushing right now with their
Prime account. They offer free two-day shipping, one-
click buying, and a subscribe-and-save program that allows
you to order staples on auto-ship with deep discounts and
the convenience of home delivery. (As a bonus, Prime
account holders can also instantly stream hundreds of free
movies and TV shows right to their computers or televi-
sions.) Mill around a Best Buy or another big box retailer
and watch the foot traffic and chat up the people you meet.
You might be shocked to discover how many of them now
use these stores as virtual show rooms for Amazon, especially with the new Amazon scan app.

A sampling of some of the other issues those retailers
will need to address:

- Supermarkets, health food stores, and big box stores
  will need to invest in and strengthen store brands

because their declining market share will require bigger profit margins.

- As the pace of life becomes increasingly hectic, people will more readily pay for convenience. Supermarkets with floral departments, bakeries, cafes, and pharmacies are probably just the beginning. Whether they will also include child-care centers, nail salons, day spas, and virtual reality holo-suites remains to be seen. Then they'll have to factor in the virtual store angle, as Tesco has done.

- Both physical and online retailers will need to figure out a way to handle delivery for the automatic orders placed by smart appliances.

- Physical retailers will need to get good at offering SMS updates with special offers and premiums for foot traffic, as well as for cars or landspeeders cruising by.

- Both online and physical retailers will have to deal with the seven billion people who subscribe to *The My Network*, and who will be ordering lots of content and won't want any advertising in it.

Once again, it will be about the experience. Physical retailers will have to work harder on what customers *experience* in their stores. Most people have a coffeemaker at home, so why do they go to Starbucks? It's really easy to buy computers and electronics online, so why do people eagerly trek to the Apple store?

It's just the opposite for online merchants. They need to emulate a model like the Mall of the America, a shopping center located in Minnesota that has over 30 million visitors a year. People drive from many miles away just to shop there, often at the same chain stores they have in their hometown. They do it because they can also ice skate, ride a roller-coaster, visit the aquarium, walk through the Nickelodeon Universe, or see the 34-foot-tall robot in the Lego store at the Mall of America.

Contrary to what the great philosopher Yogi Berra once proclaimed, people go there because that *is* the place where people go. There is a social proof and tribal element of retailing that cannot be ignored.

Why do teenage girls hang out at the mall on Saturdays? Because that's where the teenage boys hang out. Why do teenage boys hang out at the mall on Saturdays? Because that's where the teenage girls hang out.

Picture this scenario: It's Saturday morning and you need to buy a rake, some socks, and a clock. So you head out to the mega mall like you usually do. You pull into the lot and there are no cars there. You think about it, and you're sure it's not a holiday. You get that coveted space, the first one next to the handicapped ones, right by the front door.

You walk in the mall, and all the lights are on. All the stores are open with people working there. There are just no customers. This should be your dream scenario—a perfect parking spot and no other shoppers to contend with. But what would happen next would belie that . . .

Because you would probably grab what you needed and get out of there as fast as possible. It would just feel creepy. You would wonder *why* no one else was there and whether you should be there. Did something happen? Is there news you don't know about? If someone asked you about the mall later, you'd tell them not to go there, because no one goes there anymore. You need the *social proof* of other people shopping there to make you feel comfortable to shop there yourself.

People go to stores and malls because those are the places that people go to. So the challenge for online retailers will be creating vortal sites (virtual online portals), and even more so, apps that people want to spend time on, because that's where everyone hangs out.

It's still going to be about the three Cs: content, commerce, and community. But the definitions of these are changing. Here's the question you'll want to ask: How do I create the Mall of America in cyberspace?

Like many situations, the real winners may be the entrepreneurs who come from outside the space, because people in the status quo can't see beyond it.

In the book *Flash Foresight*, author Dan Burrus relates a fascinating story of speaking to the National Booksellers Association in 1993. He predicted that within two to three years, a huge, successful virtual bookstore would open that would transform the way people shopped for books. He suggested it could be one of the members present, but likely would not be, because they were already invested in the brick-and-mortar store model.

No one in the room took him seriously because most of them hardly knew the web existed. But it was only two years later when an outsider named Jeff Bezos launched Amazon.com.

When is the last time you looked at your business and your industry as an outsider would? What decisions would you make if you weren't biased by investments or processes you already had in place?

Eighty-eight million baby boomers are entering their retirement years. People are living longer and retiring later. What challenges will that create and what opportunities will it present?

The hectic pace of work and life will continue to accelerate. What challenges will that create and what opportunities will it present?

That hectic pace means that fake foods, fast foods, frozen foods, and microwaved foods will continue to increase as a percentage of our diets, which in turn means high cholesterol, heart disease, obesity, and diabetes will continue to increase. What challenges will that create and what opportunities will it present?

Those health challenges and the explosion of pharmaceuticals and medical care will likely cause a backlash and drive a renaissance toward natural foods and healthy living at some point. What challenges will that create and what opportunities will it present?

At some point, all this technology and 24-hour-a-day electronic connection and stimulation will get old, and people will hunger for an unplugged lifestyle. What challenges will that create and what opportunities will it present?

We will continue to mix marriages and blend races, eventually getting to a standardized brownish race across the globe. What challenges will that create and what opportunities will it present?

Someday soon, another planet that supports human life will be within distance through space travel and people will start migrating there. What challenges will that create and what opportunities will it present?

How can you move fast and what can you break?

Act IV

Harnessing the Ego
for Success

There is a fascinating section in *The Master Key to Riches* where Napoleon Hill lists the items required from the periodic table of elements to construct the human body and estimates what it would cost to buy them. Even with today's inflated prices, you can probably still replace yourself for less than 20 bucks. Or at least you can replace that housing that you're walking around in. So what really separates you from that $20 worth of ingredients you can purchase from the science supply website?

I would suggest *consciousness*, which leads us to an even more fascinating question: What makes us conscious of consciousness?

The ego.

Your ego is really what separates you from the elements that comprise your physical body. It is your sense of judgment, defense, and memory. It helps you organize your thoughts and make sense of the world around you. Yet conventional wisdom says the ego is bad. It has been characterized as everything from **e**dging **G**od **o**ut, to running amok, to actually being the devil.

Yet when you look at Hill's magnum opus, *Think and Grow Rich*, a mesmerizing realization jumps out at you: The people on whom he did his powerful 20-year study— a cross section of the most successful people in the world—all had strong egos.

From Ford to Firestone, Wrigley to Wannamaker, Bell to Edison, Schwab to Carnegie, Woolworth to

Rockefeller—they were powerful, strong-willed, confident people. People with healthy egos.

The New Billionaires

Fast forward to some of the most successful entrepreneurs of our time: Bill Gates, Steve Jobs, Mark Cuban, Richard Branson, Meg Whitman, Michael Dell, Ross Perot, Mark Zuckerberg, Larry Ellison, and Oprah Winfrey.

Have you ever heard any of them accused of being egoless?

If we leave the world of entrepreneurs and look at politics, sports, or even the arts, we see the same pattern: High-level achievers have a strong ego. You can make a pretty convincing argument that a powerful ego is required for powerful success.

Yes, we all know people with an inflated sense of self, but that's not what the ego really is. An easy way to discern egomania is by the desire to control others. When you're trying to control others, that's a sure sign of an *unhealthy* ego. Likewise, when you see someone always talking about how great and amazing they are, that's an ego running out of control. And it's not because they're cocky or confident. In reality it's just the opposite.

Narcissism and self-absorption come from insecurity. People who are always boasting about themselves to convey confidence are actually insecure. They don't have a healthy ego, and are acting that way to hide their fears.

People with a strong, well-balanced ego want to be great. They don't have to brag about it or look for validation from others. That's because people with strong egos are usually their own strongest critics. Their drive is internal and intense. They see stepping into their greatness as the natural progression of their path in life. For them, it's about getting to that next level of development, and they're comfortable with being recognized for that. They don't make it all about them, and certainly they get involved in service and contribution, as we'll discuss in a moment. But a strong ego is necessary for high levels of success and prosperity.

To really step into your true potential and do something epic, you must lose the perception that ego is about vanity or self-love. Instead, understand the real ego is simply the part of your mind that controls consciousness.

Let me suggest something that will cause consternation with some, but I absolutely know to be true:

The desire to be great and to be recognized for being great is healthy.

Anything less is living a life of mediocrity, and to accept mediocrity is simply not an option for people with a healthy ego.

Just doing enough to get by or taking up permanent residence on a plateau of comfort would be turning their back on their potential. And that would be an affront to everything meaningful to them, from their self-esteem to their creator.

Doing something great requires having a strong ego. The key is controlling your ego instead of it controlling you. When you take charge and direct your ego, it can play an important role in achieving your purpose in life and helping you reach great accomplishments. This necessitates becoming "the thinker of the thought" and consciously developing and controlling your ego to create the kind of life and success and prosperity you want.

I saw a fascinating interview with Mike Krzyzewski, who is coaching the latest version of the Dream Team, the USA Olympic basketball squad. He was asked how he gets these superstar athletes to check their egos at the door. His answer was quite illuminating . . . He said he didn't expect or want his players to check their egos at the door. In fact he desires his players to have ego, but he wants them to channel that personal ego into the team ego. That holds a powerful lesson for us all.

How Geniuses Harness Ego

There is much to be learned from how genius entrepreneurs channel and harness their ego to attain results. Here's an excerpt of what Napoleon Hill says on the subject in *The Master Key to Riches*:

> An Edison develops and guides his ego in the field of creative investigation and the world finds a genius whose worth cannot be estimated in dollars alone.
>
> A Henry Ford guides his ego in the field of automotive transportation and gives it such a stupendous value that it changes the trend of civilization by removing frontiers and converting mountain trails into public highways.
>
> A Marconi magnetizes his ego with a keen desire to harness the ether and lives to see his wireless communication system evolve into the discovery of the radio through which the world becomes akin, through instantaneous exchange of thought.

These men, and all others who have contributed to the march of progress, have given the world a demonstration of the power of a well-developed and carefully controlled ego.

One of the major differences between men who make valuable contributions to mankind and those who merely take up space in the world is mainly a difference in egos because the ego is the driving force behind all forms of human action.

Liberty and freedom of body and mind, the two major desires of all people, are available in exact proportion to the development and use one makes of the ego. Every person who is properly related himself to his own ego has both liberty and freedom in whatever proportions he desires.

A couple things jump out about that excerpt. The first thing you might have noticed is he is speaking exclusively about men. That's simply a reflection of the bias of the times. Today we find both men and women at every level of the workforce, so the point he makes applies to both genders. Were he writing that book today, you'd certainly have no problem envisioning Oprah in that discussion.

The other important thing about Hill's insights is the focus upon the positive results produced. In each case he is referring to the "valuable contributions to mankind" that resulted. Even more interesting is to hear Hill, one of the most positive people of his generation, use the language "taking up space" to describe a certain type of person. He's using the term to illustrate the contrast between people with an unhealthy ego versus driven people with a healthy one.

The Ego for Good

A critical element of a healthy ego is making a conscious decision to do good. If your ego is just about being recognized, getting on TV or the big screen at Times Square, that's not what we're talking about.

It is a sign of the disease of our society today that there are so many people who are famous simply for being famous. That leads to notoriety, and a savvy manipulator can milk that attention for a certain degree of money. But it will never bring the lasting success we're concerned with here. This kind of superficial pursuit of attention isn't based on anything of value. And all true prosperity is based on providing value; each interaction is a value-for-value exchange.

Lasting success can also never come from exploiting people or plundering resources. It's about creating win/win scenarios that benefit both parties. To be in congruence with these universal laws of success, as you develop your ego you must be mindful about contributing, not just receiving.

So what constitutes a healthy ego? And how do you actually take charge of the process and develop your ego to drive you to success?

There are six steps in the process. Here's the list. We'll look at each one in turn:

1. Direct your ego to a higher purpose.
2. Pursue your purpose with passion.
3. Think critically and consciously.
4. Take continuous action.
5. Guide your ego through self-discipline.
6. Develop a support group.

Step 1: Direct Your Ego to a Higher Purpose

When you work toward a higher purpose, you elevate your own consciousness and that of everyone around you. You attract people to your vision, and they help keep you grounded and moving forward.

My friend Ian Percy is a seminal critical thinker on the subject of purpose, and consults with companies seeking to perform better. One of the things he says in his book *The Profitable Power of Purpose* is "the national epidemic is that people look for 'jobs' not for 'purpose.' We should stop measuring the 'jobless rate' and start measuring the 'purposeless rate.'" Not very practical, perhaps, but this statement does give us much food for thought.

Think about it. Chasing a paycheck or a stock price doesn't really inspire anyone long-term. Following your life's purpose not only inspires you to daily action, but it gets you out of yourself. As you move along your path, your purpose naturally moves toward the higher realms.

You still want to make money, get a promotion, or create a profitable venture, but you view those desires through the lens of creating true value, which inherently leads to more enlightened pursuits.

Step 2: Pursue Your Purpose with Passion

When you have the right purpose, you're going to become passionate about that purpose. You're going to want to see it achieved and make it happen. Your subconscious mind pulls you toward it.

If your ego is out of control and your purpose is simply "I want to get a Lamborghini," you may approach that with passion because you really want that Lamborghini. But a purpose so superficial isn't really going to inspire you to the long-term success you're looking for.

As we'll discuss in the next act, purpose starts with getting your own needs met first. But as you grow, your purpose starts to be more about service. It still requires taking care of your own needs, but now your needs are about the joy that comes from serving others, the joy that comes from contribution. So it's selfish, but it's selfish in a very positive way.

Step 3: Think Critically and Consciously

We've been exploring this in depth throughout the book, so I won't belabor it here. You will find that the number of people who practice critical thinking is shockingly low. Let's go back to something fascinating that Dan Burrus discusses in *Flash Foresight*.

He relates the story of how the Baby Boomer generation has been aging and creating demands along the way. First, there weren't enough diaper services, then there weren't enough preschools and primary schools. Next, there weren't enough high schools and then universities. You've heard this story before, I'm sure, and you know how the boomers have impacted the world as they reached their thirties, forties, and fifties. *But here's the really fascinating part* . . . Not only was the market not prepared as they progressed through the decades, but it still isn't prepared! The elder care, retirement, and funeral industries don't yet have enough capacity for the onslaught of demand they are facing. The need is as predictable as the seasons, and they've had more than five decades to prepare, but most all of the industries that stand to benefit tremendously from the baby boomers are still not ready for it.

They are stuck in the model of reacting to demand instead of being critical thinkers and anticipating it.

Don't make the same mistake. Question the status quo. Use critical thinking and start playing the chess match a few moves ahead.

Step 4: Take Continuous Action

Another thing Hill discusses in *The Master Key to Riches* is cosmic habit force. In practical terms this means the daily habits that create your results.

Successful people are people in motion. They move a step closer to their dream daily. They are in action every day, even when they don't feel like it. This takes motivation.

Because I'm a professional speaker and I talk about success, people usually position me as a motivational speaker. As a result, I often get asked about the secrets of motivation. Here's what might be the most effective one:

Incremental progress Nothing inspires you more or causes you to motivate yourself more than actually seeing yourself getting closer to your dream. (Except when your dream is too timid and doesn't excite you. But that's another book . . .)

Success Is Not a Microwave, but a Crock-Pot, and Your Daily Habits Are the Ingredients If you need to lose 60 pounds, working out at the gym isn't a lot of fun.

But if you lose seven pounds the first week, you'll get excited. You start to believe your goal may be attainable. You exercise a little longer after getting the good news on the scale. Each week you make some more progress. Now you're actually increasing muscle and decreasing fat. Your metabolism goes up and weight starts to fall off faster. You get even more motivated and your incremental progress pulls you toward your goal.

Let's suppose you're deeply in debt. If you're like most people in this situation, you don't want to know the particulars and you deal with bills only as you have to. A better strategy would be taking a complete inventory of your obligations, seeing exactly where you are, and setting up a payoff schedule. The key is tracking the progress and seeing your debt get smaller every week. That progress keeps you motivated.

It Works the Other Way, Too Let's suppose you're focused on building your net worth. One of the best things to do is have your accountant prepare a monthly financial statement for you. Whether you're trying to eliminate debt or create wealth, seeing regular progress toward your goal has the effect of pulling you toward it. This motivates you and leads us to . . .

Step 5: Guide Your Ego Through Self-Discipline

When you're in continuous action and beginning to see incremental progress, you feel motivated. This is not external rah-rah motivation, but the very best kind: powerful motivation from within. This motivation helps you create self-discipline, and that drives the daily actions, which will take you where you want to go.

When you're motivated—moving forward and taking daily action—you harness your ego to produce the outcome you desire. This structure provides a guide for your ego, and it then works subconsciously to drive you toward your goals.

The Irony Paradox   It's ironic that many people hate discipline because discipline creates freedom.

As a general rule, successful people work harder than others. They simply work more hours. But they also do something else: They manage what they do during those hours better than most. They have learned the difference between busywork and rainmaker activities. They practice self-discipline, keeping themselves focused on productive activities. They do this by making choices, which sometimes means making sacrifices. Because this much is certain: *If you want to reach a high level of success, there will be many things you will have to eliminate from your life.*

Some of the things you sacrifice are simply distractions. Some are pleasant diversions. And some are activities you actually love and wish to keep doing, but you will make a conscious choice to sacrifice them in deference to the main purpose in your life. You give up some things you want to get the things you *really want*.

Certainly we know successful people manage their time effectively, but there are a lot of other things they also manage well. And they do this through self-restraint.

It's all about the choices you make, the priorities you set, and deciding what is really important in terms of reaching your purpose in life. And the thing that really comes into play here is your energy. The secret to harnessing your ego is using self-control to transmute energy into a desired purpose.

People often complain about their energy level, like it was bestowed upon or withheld from them by some mystical external source. But, of course, you are in control of your energy. Successful people don't find energy. They know full well that it is created internally.

Your energy and vitality are a result of the choices you make.

By the food you eat (or don't), the rest you give yourself (or don't), the weight you carry around (or don't), and the vices you abstain from (or don't).

Adding by Subtracting The process is both physical and mental. You increase your energy by abstaining from self-indulgence. And you improve your harmony and reasoning by shunning distractions and time wasters like worry, jealousy, and envy.

You may like ice cream, pizza, and pasta (like I do), but if you give in to those urges too often, physically you're going to be overweight, lethargic, and weak. Likewise, if you're throwing away your harmony with thoughts of revenge, hate, and jealousy, you're certainly not going to be focused on your next million-dollar idea. When you control your body and thoughts you will be calm, collected, and have the energy to tackle any challenge you face.

No discussion of harnessing ego and self-discipline and how they lead you to success would be complete without exploring the issue of channeling sexual energy.

Sexual energy is one of the most powerful forces on earth. In *Think and Grow Rich*, Napoleon Hill suggests that the reason most men don't reach higher levels of success until their fifties is because it takes them that long to harness their sexual energy.

As Woody Allen once famously said, "Even the worst orgasm I ever had was pretty good!" But if you have ever studied chi (life force), you know every time a male ejaculates, he depletes his chi. That is why practitioners of tantric sex often experience orgasm without ejaculation. For most people, abstinence is not required or even desirable. However, moderation and discernment can help you channel that energy into pursuits of excellence in other areas.

Just as was true with some of the other things we've discussed, there will be times you have to give up some habits you want to get what you really want. Moderation and self-restraint mean avoiding the unnecessary, practicing moderation in indulgences, and completely abstaining from the things that are actually harmful.

You're not that different from anyone else; you appreciate recognition and rewards. So another way to keep yourself focused on a positive path is to set benchmark goals with an appropriate reward for each one. That could mean anything from getting a massage when you finish writing a book chapter (as I'll be doing shortly) to buying yourself a Ferrari when you book a certain amount of new business.

Step 6: Develop a Support Group

We all need people who will call us on our stuff. It's only natural that as you work your way up the success ladder, your confidence will grow and you'll be pleased with who you are becoming. That's a good thing. High-level achievers are usually comfortable in their own skin.

But when you enjoy success after success and receive enough accolades, it's easy to go over to the dark side, so developing a support group is important. You need people who love you, want the highest good for you, and just as importantly, will tell you when you get off track. This means people you can check things out with and know that they will tell you the truth.

When you look at some of the people whose lives have run amok, like Michael Jackson, Whitney Houston, Amy Winehouse, and so many others, it certainly appears that they did not have this kind of support group around them. They were all brilliant, artistic geniuses and achieved the highest levels of success in their profession, but they probably surrounded themselves with people who enabled everything they did. You can find this pattern of tortured genius in many different realms, and I've fought it myself many times. It happens when you don't surround yourself with people strong enough to confront you when they feel your future is threatened.

Even Ayn Rand, one of the most brilliant intellectuals of the last century, reached the end of her life with only a small, inner circle of devotees around her—having pushed away anyone who didn't agree with everything she said. I believe that lack of intellectual challenge hurt her.

The greatest gift you could ever give anyone is telling them the truth and being real for them. And the greatest gift you can receive from those closest to you is the same consideration.

This doesn't mean being negative, attacking people, or tearing them down. You've got to find people who will do it with love and for your highest good, and if you get two or three people in the world who you can trust, you're doing wonderful. If you find five or six, you're doing amazing. (And if you do find five or six, you have the opportunity to start a Mastermind group and experience all of the benefits such a group offers.)

If you create the right support group around you, this will greatly assist you in harnessing your ego in a powerful and positive way.

A balanced ego is always under the control of the individual. Either you control your ego or your ego controls you. If you're uncertain whether or not you are in control, the right support group will help you know the truth.

The Role of the Ego to Manifest Prosperity

Harnessing your ego to create success is a process of connecting your conscious mind with your subconscious mind. Your subconscious mind doesn't rationalize, analyze, or critique. It just does what it's programmed to do. But when the conscious mind isn't in alignment with your subconscious mind, you have a conflict. You have a conscious mind that might say something like, "I want to be a millionaire," but you could have subconscious programming that money is bad or rich people are evil. When conflicts like these arise, the subconscious mind always wins! It can cause you to self-sabotage your own success. (And often does.)

To develop a healthy ego you must get your conscious and subconscious minds in alignment. To do this, it's helpful to see how you got out of alignment, then simply reverse-engineer the process.

If I have learned anything about success and prosperity, it is the process that causes people to create results. It's comprised of four very simple, but very profound truths:

1. Your current reality is a result of the daily actions you've taken up to this point.

2. Your habits are determined by your subconscious mind, based on the vision you have for yourself.

3. Your vision is the result of your core, foundational beliefs.

4. Your core, foundational beliefs are the result of the programming you are exposed to.

There are three main sources for programming, most of it negative:

1. Government

2. Organized religion

3. The data-sphere (media, social media, friends, family)

The Really Frightening Part   Most, if not all, of your core, foundational beliefs about prosperity were set before you reached 10 years of age. If your parents fought all the time, that created your belief about relationships. If your father cheated on your mother, that solidified your beliefs about marriage. And it's a very safe bet that most of the programming you received about money was the usual negative variety: money is bad, rich people are evil, you sell your soul for money, it's spiritual to be poor, and so on.

So what happens?

You think you want to be rich and successful, but on a subconscious level, you believe that rich people are bad. You apply for a better position, open a new business, or start after some other worthy goal. Your subconscious immediately kicks into gear to protect your ego. It tells you that you don't want to be one of those evil, mean rich people, so you better stop doing what you're doing right away. It causes you to change your actions, and you actually sabotage your own success.

Millions of people around the world are stuck in this self-defeating cycle of sabotage. Consciously they want success, but subconsciously they think it's wrong to even try. And remember, your subconscious mind always wins.

The ego is very fertile soil for creating doubt and fear—or developing faith and belief. You have to be the one who determines which. This goes back to being the thinker of the thought or, put another way, thinking about what you think about. You must become aware of the people and environment around you and the kind of programming you're receiving from them.

To create success, you start at the bottom and work back. You must first take control of the programming you allow yourself to be exposed to. That means sometimes limiting the movies, programs, and even people you are exposed to. And it means that when you know you're receiving negative programming, you consciously counter-program with something positive.

When you have the majority of your programming is positive, it changes your core, foundational beliefs. Having different, more-empowering beliefs allows you to set a higher vision for yourself. Your subconscious mind (the ego) drives you to practice daily habits that take you closer to your vision, and those actions produce a better result.

Staying in Balance

The well-balanced ego doesn't get dragged out of context by compliments or condemnation. Neither one of those extremes is really going to affect you unduly. When somebody compliments you, you'll accept it, appreciate it, and thank them. If people attack you, you take it in, consider the source and motivation, and if need be, check it out with your support group. In either event you're going to keep moving toward your purpose.

Be a Contrarian   Most people today doubt their beliefs and believe their doubts—don't. Once you have discerned your purpose and follow the steps we've discussed, your ego will naturally channel your energy toward the completion of your mission. Then it's about removing fear factors and doubts. Some of this may come from reducing your exposure to negative people. Be mindful of other people's opinions of you. Don't let their limiting beliefs become yours. You must also be more mindful of the programming you're allowing yourself to become exposed to. You have to be a contrarian and question everything. Just because people have titles, degrees, or positions of authority doesn't mean they are always right. They frequently are not. Always check the premise.

Do you really believe the airlines when they tell you that your cell phone causes problems for the plane's navigation system, but the $2-a-minute service they sell you doesn't? I don't.

Do you believe your government when they say that they want to raise a sales tax temporarily to pay for a capital improvement, and they'll reduce it after that's done? I don't.

You might think if a city needed someone to design their airport, they would commission an architect who had actually been in one, but obviously Madrid, Spain, didn't. (I couldn't confirm this at press time, but I believe J.K. Rowling's idea for the moving stairways at Hogwarts was inspired by the Madrid jetways.)

You probably also think if an airport needed a new terminal, they would hire people to build it who could do so without the ceiling collapsing and killing passengers. But the Charles-de-Gaulle Airport didn't.

Back in the 1970s, our counter-culture heroes like Jagger, Dylan, and Townsend famously warned to never trust anyone over 30. They're about double that now, but I still trust them more than I do the government. (And come to think of it, I never did get those flashbacks they promised me!)

Airline executives believe that a hub-and-spoke system is a feasible way to run an airline. They believe that because someone theorized it, some airline did it, and lots of others followed suit. But there's no rational evidence to suggest it's financially viable.

You might think a general contractor would check the plumbing and electrical connections before he put expensive Italian tile on a wall. But if you do—you never hired the one I did.

Just because someone went to college, studied a lot of books on economic theory, and came out with a PhD in economics doesn't mean they actually understand how it works in the real world. People who can't balance their own checkbook should not be setting government financial policies.

Don't get cynical. Cynics don't attract success. But be willing to be skeptical. Skeptics are critical thinkers; they readily discern negative input and disregard it. Skeptics recognize opportunities that others miss. So analyze all of the programming you receive, even that from your family and friends.

Inevitably, you will be exposed to a great deal of negative programming, so it is vital that you become mindful of it, and program a larger amount of positive programming to weigh the scale in your favor. This means taking actions like finding a good Mastermind group, employing autosuggestion with affirmations, and creating dream boards. It also includes reading, watching, and listening to empowering and inspirational books, videos, and audios. Fear and faith cannot coexist. When you feel fear, profess faith. The prosperity manifestation formula is a simple one:

1. Plant seeds with positive programming.
2. Water with repetition.
3. Harvest.

Everybody's ego changes every day. Yours is always undergoing changes for better or worse because of the nature of your thoughts. In *As A Man Thinketh*, James Allen uses the analogy of our minds as a garden, which can be intelligently cultivated or allowed to run wild. In either event, it will bring forth something.

If you plant and tend your garden, it will produce flowers or fruits, the things you cultivate. If you don't plant specific seeds, then animals, wind, and other elements will cause random things to fall into it, producing an abundance of weeds and wild vegetation, likely to choke out useful plants. One thing is certain: Something will grow in your garden.

Just as a gardener must tend his or her plot by keeping out the weeds, you must tend the garden of your mind, weeding out the thoughts of lack, limitation, and negativity. You must nurture and tend the thoughts of happiness, success, and purpose.

If you practice gardening of this kind, you will soon discover that you are the master gardener of your success. You will come to the profound revelation that you are not the victim of your circumstances, but the architect of them. That the thoughts you give precedence to will shape your character, create your circumstances, and determine your ultimate destiny.

Control the thoughts you give precedence to and you'll always be moving closer to your goals. You will have a well-balanced ego that can be harnessed for greatness!

Soprano Aria

Selfishness Is the
New Altruism

ere's something they probably didn't teach you in Sunday school . . . or business school:

Your highest moral purpose must be your own success and happiness.

If you think that means I'm advocating selling your soul, exploiting others, or becoming a narcissist, I'm not. I am saying that making your own success and happiness your highest purpose is the only healthy, sane way to live. And it's the only way that ensures the survival of the species and the well-being of the most people. In fact, it is the only honorable way to conduct any relationship, business or personal.

Your highest good must form the foundation of your value system. To make your life, by your own means, according to your own standards, and for your own enjoyment. Anything less than that is harmful to you. And anything harmful to the individual is actually detrimental to society as a whole.

That doesn't mean you won't sometimes sacrifice or subjugate your own needs for others in a relationship, or as parents do for their children quite frequently. The real issue is when that becomes the norm: When you see serving and helping others as more important than helping yourself. It's a sure sign of low self-esteem, worthiness issues, and harmful mind viruses—and that is the fastest way to a life of victimhood, resentment, and frustration.

To be able to give, you must have.

—Mother Teresa

121

When your own success and happiness is your purpose, you have a productive—and moral—reason to exist. And here's the important thing:

If everyone did this, the world would be a much better place!

Instead of dysfunction, depravity, and codependence, we would have healthy, functional, value-for-value relationships. No one would be asking you to sacrifice for him or her, and you would not ask others to sacrifice for you. That is the way healthy relationships are formed, the way healthy transactions are completed, and the way to conduct business with integrity.

If you tell me your highest good is serving others or even serving God, I think you've lost the plot. In my experience those running around trying to save the world are usually the most messed up people you'll ever meet. Their lives are usually driven by avoidance behavior so they don't have to deal with their own issues. They run around looking for drama, so they don't have time to face their own drama. To the casual observer they look like altruistic saints, but those who know better recognize them for the judgmental, insecure, drama-magnets they really are. At their core, they are desperately looking for acceptance. They think if they rescue enough other people, this will somehow give them the self-esteem they're missing. It won't.

You have to get comfortable in your own skin. No one else can give you that validation. Get yourself in a position of strength and you'll be amazed how much good you can do.

Selfish Is Good   Of course, you'll discover that you do that good for selfish reasons.

If you live your life by the principles we are discussing, you very well may help others and contribute to charity. Hopefully you do. Personally, the number-one deduction on my tax return for the last 15 years has been charity, and I anticipate that it will remain so for the rest of my life. But there are three criteria I look for:

1. The person or organization is worthy of the support.
2. I can afford to do it.
3. It brings me happiness to do it.

That alone is what determines where I spend my charity dollars. It certainly has nothing to do with who is the neediest or what causes are politically correct.

I support a great deal of causes: The opera, runaway shelters, the symphony, my church, wildlife funds, disease prevention and cures, homeless shelters, scholarships, computers for aspiring entrepreneurs, stage clothes for upcoming singers, and martial arts training for foster kids, sponsorships for amateur sports teams, and holiday presents for hundreds of kids who otherwise wouldn't have received any.

But I do all this for purely selfish reasons, for the happiness it brings me.

And that is where this all leads to. You know exactly what brings value to you and furthers your purpose, which is a life of happiness. It means accepting that you are supposed to be happy and working toward that end without shame, because you refuse to give in to guilt rackets that are practiced on you.

This is not to be confused with hedonism. The philosophy of hedonism holds that only what is pleasant or has pleasant consequences is intrinsically good. The psychology of hedonism holds that all behavior is motivated by the desire for pleasure and the avoidance of pain. I'm not advocating either.

Simply lusting after pleasure all the time with no regard for the consequences won't make you happy. In fact, that course will certainly lead to unhappiness, and that kind of instant gratification and self-indulgence will take you away from success, not toward it.

Now this is where the beginning success seeker can become very confused, because while we are discussing doing things for the greater good, we're not talking about being selfless. In fact, it's just the opposite. We're talking about being selfish.

Ayn Rand is best known for her amazing works, *Atlas Shrugged* and *The Fountainhead*, but her most insightful book may be the lesser-known *The Virtue of Selfishness: A New Concept of Egoism*. Published in 1964, it is a collection of essays woven together for their insights on the philosophy of Objectivism, the nature of a proper government, egoism as a rational code of ethics, and the potential dark side of altruism.

Rand's characterization of selfishness as a virtue brought immediate controversy. When asked why she would choose to use the word selfishness in such a context, she replied to the questioner that she did so for the very reason it scared him.

In the book's introduction, Rand acknowledges that the word selfishness isn't usually used to describe virtuous behavior, but she insists that this usage is a more accurate definition of the term as simply "a concern with one's own interests."

Like Rand, I also use the word selfish to describe virtuous qualities of character. I take it to mean you value yourself first, regardless of what anyone else thinks. Notice that there is no good or evil implicit in the definition. It simply means that you are well adjusted and sensible enough to meet your own needs first.

Now of course that's not what most people would have you believe . . .

The collectivism movement sweeping the globe today would have you believe that it is your moral imperative to put the interests of the many before the needs of the one—that you should sacrifice yourself for the greater good. This idea may look good on the surface, but it is actually quite dangerous and will lead you away from success, instead of toward it. Because *we* all are the greatest good.

Self-sacrifice is more than the root of low self-esteem; it is anti–free enterprise and consequently anti-humanity. When the living energy of productive citizens is sucked from them by well-meaning but ultimately malicious entitlement programs, there is no incentive to remain productive. All innovation and development stop and everyone loses.

Millions of mind viruses generated by the media, organized religion, and the government are swirling around, telling you to be selfless and take care of others. And if you buy into this crazy philosophy, you are doomed to a life of lack, misery, and frustration—of unrealized dreams and settling for mediocrity. You have to think differently, way differently.

Living a life of self-sacrifice enables others to take advantage of you and, when practiced long enough, will ultimately destroy you. You have no purpose in life, other than placating others and seeking their approval, which you can earn only by giving up your own happiness. This is sick, twisted, and dysfunctional.

Every time I discuss this, someone trots out the examples of Mother Teresa, Gandhi, and so on, as though that somehow negated the logic of the argument. It doesn't. They both acted in total alignment with their own values and sense of self, and you can see that their "selfishness" benefited millions of people.

If you see your main purpose in life as serving others, you have an extremely low opinion of yourself. You won't believe you are worthy and will experience a tremendous amount of lack and limitation in your life, not to mention you'll probably be personally responsible for the founding of at least three chapters of Codependents Anonymous!

Insanity is a lack of reason or good sense. We could certainly define it as unsoundness of mind rendering a person unfit to maintain a relationship or look after his or her own needs for emotional well-being and survival. People who spend their existence worrying solely about the needs of others and not themselves are not noble, benevolent, and spiritual. They are just crazy. And to quote Melvin Udall, Jack Nicholson's character from the movie, *As Good As It Gets*, "Go sell crazy somewhere else; we're all stocked up here."

People who don't look after their own needs first, really can't help others in a healthy way. They can console them, participate in their drama, or enable their codependence, but they can't offer them real, meaningful help.

Want to save the world? Great, it needs all the help it can get. Start by making sure your own needs are met first. Get the money thing out of the way. Get yourself in a position of strength—and you'll be amazed how much good you can do!

Your Purpose Can Pull You Forward

In the beginning, your purpose is not to serve God or save the world. (Although at some point that may become the case.) Your purpose must be following the path to reach your potential. Which, by the way, is the *best* way to serve God and what God wants most from and for you. Your purpose must entail getting your own needs met first and evolving into the best person you can be.

This is not about using people, taking advantage of others, or just grabbing what you want for yourself. It is about making sure your own needs are met, walking your path, and then seeing where that leads you. And as you know from the previous acts, the greatest opportunities are the ones that solve challenges for other people.

Finding Your Path

To reach success requires that you discover the path you are meant to walk. It is the challenge you were placed here to solve. This though, is just the first step. Once you solve that challenge, the next one will appear. And that challenge won't show up until you are overqualified for the first one. Success is simply a continuous process of conquering challenges.

It's not about judging or comparing. Your first path might be meeting the need of your local Domino's Pizza store for a delivery driver. Begin where you are and grow from there.

As your consciousness evolves, so will your challenges.

If you are at a stage in life where you're wondering the path for you, seek for clues by asking yourself:

What do I love?

What makes me cry?

What is the injustice I want to right?

Finding the things you really care about offers great clues to where your path may lead. However, it's only fair to warn you what may happen when you find your path.

It may require sacrifice, and often does. The universe will test you to see if you are serious. You even may be attacked, ridiculed, or ostracized for the path you take. Now if *all* those things happen—you've probably found your true path!

As your challenges progress, they deepen into your purpose, and your purpose pulls you forward. Every problem exists only because a possibility exists. If the possibility were not there, neither would the problem. *And this is where an important process takes place: that of moving from self-consciousness to cosmic consciousness.*

We all begin at self-consciousness. The focus here is on you and your personality, which must be protected at

all costs. You're a slave to desire and want instant gratification. You're chasing the next raise, next promotion, or
next job. At this stage, selfishness means getting something before someone else gets it first.

As you practice daily self-development, your conscious
grows from self-consciousness to cosmic consciousness. At
this stage you've learned to master your desires and enjoy
the journey.

It's not that you forsake all pleasure: It is just no
longer an end in itself. It is transmuted. (Just as we discussed with sexual energy.) You receive gratification, but
it is purified and experienced through the right thoughts
and actions. Now you are meeting your own needs, and as
a result, are able to help many others. You graduate to
service and contribution—still through the prism of
selfishness—however, it is enlightened selfishness.

At this stage, you get more joy from sponsoring an
opera than you receive from buying a Ferrari. You may
still buy the Ferrari, but your enjoyment is enhanced by
driving it to the opening gala of the opera production that
you sponsored.

For companies, this is when they evolve from just
beating last year's profit margins to looking at ways they
can continue to grow, while preserving the environment,
improving working conditions, rewarding critical thinkers,
and fostering innovation. When people and companies
think selfishly, they ultimately produce more value.

As Ian Percy says in *The Profitable Power of Purpose*:

You need both economy (money) and ecology
(meaning) in everything you do. My opinion is that,

before anything else, you need an ecological statement of purpose. This is the purpose that makes
whatever you are doing worth doing.

This is what lights the fire in the belly and puts
the sparkle in the eyes. This is what unites and inspires
the entire organization to do something grand and
transformative. This is like falling in love with your
work and your work falling in love with you. You
don't just have a purpose, the purpose has you.

When working with companies, Ian's first admonition
is simple: *You can't have peak performance without first having
a peak purpose.* For people and companies—and companies
are simply people in collaboration—an enlightened self-
interest in pursuit of a purpose creates magic.

At some point, while chasing success, you'll reach a
stage where no amount of cars, cash, or homes will satisfy
you. That's because money and material things don't
provide happiness. Money and material things do allow
you self-expression, which provides happiness.

But when your self-expression is only about you and
scoring more points than anyone else, the victory is a
shallow one. You'll reach a stage where you will hunger
for something with more meaning. You understand that
prosperity isn't really about reaching success, but living a
successful life.

Even companies reach a stage where success has to
become about more than better dividends, bigger market
share, and squashing the competition. Companies take on
the culture of their leaders and as the consciousness of the
leaders develops, so will the culture.

The Path to Prosperity

The path to prosperity is making the natural transition from success to significance.

That's the real journey from self-consciousness to cosmic consciousness. Great Teachers of many ages all taught this, although they each used different words to describe it:

Emerson: Over-Soul

Jesus: Heaven

Buddha: Nirvana

Lao-Tze: Tao

Satha Sai Baba: The Path of Love

I'm using a different label than James Allen did, and he used a different one than the Great Teachers. But we're all talking about the change of consciousness that develops in a human being who is practicing enlightened self-interest. You seek accomplishment, but not for its own sake. You seek continuous challenges and new achievements because those are the next steps of your natural evolution.

For people at this stage of enlightenment, mediocrity is a sin.

Not sin as most people define it, but in its original meaning in the Bible, to "miss the mark." Your mark is to live a life of your fullest potential. People with enlightened consciousness are driven to higher achievements and excellence because to settle for anything less than that would be denying their gifts and renouncing their own greatness.

Everyone is born with this state of consciousness. Unfortunately for many, they allow negative programming to cloud their judgment and alter their core, foundational beliefs. That's why so much of the work I do with people is about unlearning instead of learning. I do believe we all know innately that our greatness exists and is waiting to be called upon. And that's the most important risk you will ever take: daring to be great!

The After Party

Sameness Creates Comfort; Difference Creates Opportunity

As this book has progressed, I've been posting some excerpts and soliciting feedback on my blog and social media feeds. Some of the people who have followed my work for a long time have been quite perplexed about my choice of subject matter. Not a small number have asked a fascinating question: Why is a guy who is supposed to be a prosperity and success guru writing a book with all this gloom and doom?

It's a fair question in light of the little they've seen until now. Let's face it, so far I've outlined:

- Disruptive technology will eliminate millions of jobs.
- You could soon be replaced by an animal, or even a clone.
- Your government is probably run by the ethics of a Ponzi scheme.
- There could be a New World Order.
- Everything they told you about the ego is wrong.
- Selfishness is good.
- Cataclysmic change is coming.

That's all pretty earth-shattering, mind-bending stuff. Certainly some people will view all these changes with fear and trepidation. But as you've probably realized by now, these changes actually offer the greatest opportunity to create wealth in human history.

We are living in the most fascinating, extraordinary, and yes, challenging time ever. And in those challenges lie the most lucrative opportunities.

There has never been a better time to be alive. Really. There has never been a better opportunity to create success. Really.

But safe, conventional thinking doesn't work any longer. If you want to really break through in this new environment, there is no question that playing safe is now actually quite dangerous. You must be bold and break the mold. Sameness creates comfort. Difference creates opportunity.

Find Opportunity

Seek out the challenges. Determine what the problems will be and who will be facing them, because therein lie the greatest opportunities for contrarians, critical thinkers, and people willing to take risks.

Next, look for opportunities to practice leverage.

Of course, the term *leverage* comes from the action of a lever that pivots on one point and is used to move an object at a second point when a force is applied at a third. In the prosperity sense, we're using leverage to utilize a small initial investment of money, time, or effort to gain a high return on that investment. Leverage allows you to quicken your wealth building the way compound interest accelerates your savings account. Businesses that allow you to practice leverage are always superior wealth-building vehicles than linear ones.

Whether it is leveraging your money with real estate, leveraging your time through network marketing, or leveraging your knowledge as an information entrepreneur, you accelerate the speed you accumulate wealth because, all other things being equal, leverage beats trading hours for currency.

Working hard is good, but working hard at a traditional job is more likely to keep you just over broke than it is to create wealth. There are millions of jobs—and millions of businesses—where working hard all day, every day will not make you rich. You are doing a straight trade of hours for currency, and there simply are not enough hours in the day.

If Jimmy Buffet only got paid to sing "Margaritaville" live, he'd never enjoy the lifestyle he has created by recording it once and selling it millions of times. J.K. Rowling and Oprah Winfrey didn't become a couple of the wealthiest people on earth by trading physical labor for a salary; they used their creativity and harnessed the power of leverage brilliantly.

So look for problems to solve, become a critical thinker to solve them, and be mindful of opportunities to create leverage. But to become a wealthy individual or a successful business still requires one more thing . . .

A New and Different Level of Thinking

Being a contrarian certainly helps, as does understanding trends and discerning the difference between hard and soft ones. You must be thoughtful of which patterns are cyclical or linear. By using this information and doing some critical thinking, you can make some pretty certain assumptions about where the future is headed.

But it's still more than that, because what we're really talking about can best be described as *prosperity consciousness*. And that is a mindset. A mindset driven by abundance, not lack. Not the fear-of-loss mindset that most people have, but a mindset of possibilities.

The many years I have been studying the principles of prosperity have brought me to a few fascinating realizations:

- Healthy people think differently than sick people.
- Happy people think differently than depressed people.
- Wealthy people think differently than broke people.

Healthy people have more energy and find it easier to exercise. They're eating a healthier diet so they face less physiological cravings for bad stuff. People who enjoy good health have a totally different view about things like diet, exercise, and addictions than people who are sick.

Happy people face challenges just like depressed people do. But nothing has any meaning, except what we choose to give it. Depressed people might see a challenge as an insurmountable obstacle, while happy people see it as a wake-up call from the universe to make a course correction.

Take the same opportunity and offer it to a broke person and wealthy person, and I guarantee you they will see it differently. When I was poor, I looked at everything through the lens of the mind viruses I was infected with. No matter what business venture I was exposed to, I approached it with the beliefs that you need money to make money; you need an education and have to know people; and so on. I could look at anything and immediately give you 15 reasons why it wouldn't work. While I was accumulating all the evidence why it couldn't be done, people with prosperity consciousness were simply doing it.

For those many years I was struggling financially, I was a cynic. And nothing kills innovation, creativity, and ambition faster than cynicism. It's poverty consciousness.

Wealthy people have a healthy skepticism that causes them to evaluate things objectively and make good decisions based on solid assumptions. Skepticism is healthy; cynicism never is. Here's why: If you ask the wrong question, the answer doesn't matter.

For all those years when I was mired in poverty consciousness, the questions I asked were always looking for evidence to demonstrate why success wouldn't work for me. When I began to develop prosperity consciousness, the questions began to change to ones of possibilities.

As a coach now, I'm working with some of the brightest entrepreneurial minds on earth. I was also fortunate to be included in a documentary titled, *The Y.E.S. Movie* (Young Entrepreneur Society). Some of the kids featured in this film made millions while they were still in their teens. In addition, I've been blessed to meet and work with a few billionaires. Working with all these high-level achievers offers an intriguing look into their minds and specifically, how they think.

And it certainly isn't conventional.

They're savvy entrepreneurs and they're as adverse to foolish risk as anyone. The difference is *what* they perceive as risk. They know the safe route always leads to mediocrity, and that is the real risk. They know that unconventional approaches, contrarian thinking, and innovation—which sometimes means tipping things upside down, and sometimes means beginning with a blank canvas—are where the real magic is.

Every great company—and the entrepreneurs who run them—must be willing to evolve. You must be willing to let go of who you *are* to become who you are *meant to be*. That is the path to epic outcomes.

Be willing to be bold, to think laterally and creatively, to question, and to be a contrarian. Dare to be different; dare to take a risk. Because risky is the new safe!

Required Reading
for Risk Takers

Prosperity, by Charles Fillmore

The Master Key to Riches, by Napoleon Hill

Think and Grow Rich, by Napoleon Hill

Atlas Shrugged, by Ayn Rand

The Fountainhead, by Ayn Rand

The Virtue of Selfishness: A New Concept of Egoism, by Ayn Rand

Building Brand Value, by Bruce Turkel

Flash Foresight, by Daniel Burrus with John David Mann

UnMarketing, by Scott Stratten

As a Man Thinketh, by James Allen

With Purpose, by Ken Dychtwald, PhD, and Daniel J. Kadlec

Becoming a Category of One, by Joe Calloway

Connect with Randy!

Website: www.randygage.com

![t] https://twitter.com/Randy_Gage

![f] www.facebook.com/randygage

![You Tube] www.youtube.com/randygage

![e] http://empireavenue.com/RGAGE

Scan this QR code to download my Prosperity App!